Michelangelo
Painter, Sculptor, and Architect

MAKERS OF THE MIDDLE AGES AND RENAISSANCE

Michelangelo

Painter, Sculptor, and Architect

Tim McNeese

CHELSEA HOUSE
PUBLISHERS
A Haights Cross Communications Company ®
Philadelphia

COVER: Portrait of Michelangelo, by Marcello Venusti.

CHELSEA HOUSE PUBLISHERS
VP, NEW PRODUCT DEVELOPMENT Sally Cheney
DIRECTOR OF PRODUCTION Kim Shinners
CREATIVE MANAGER Takeshi Takahashi
MANUFACTURING MANAGER Diann Grasse

Staff for Michelangelo
EXECUTIVE EDITOR Lee Marcott
EDITORIAL ASSISTANT Carla Greenberg
PRODUCTION EDITOR Noelle Nardone
COVER AND INTERIOR DESIGNER Keith Trego
LAYOUT 21st Century Publishing and Communications, Inc.

A Haights Cross Communications ✦ Company ®

www.chelseahouse.com

First Printing

9 8 7 6 5 4 3 2 1

Library of Congress Cataloging-in-Publication Data

McNeese, Tim.
   Michelangelo: painter, sculptor, and architect/Tim McNeese.
      p. cm.–(Makers of the Middle Ages and Renaissance)
   Includes bibliographical references and index.
   ISBN 0-7910-8627-5 (hard cover)
 1. Michelangelo Buonarroti, 1475–1564–Juvenile literature.
 2. Artists–Italy–Biography–Juvenile literature. I. Title. II. Series.
 N6923.M45M38 2005
 709'.2–dc22
                                    2005007493

CONTENTS

A Genius
at Work

Millions of tourists travel to the European country of Italy each year to view some of history's greatest works of art. In the northern-Italian city of Florence, one of the most important and grandest centers of Renaissance art, visitors can tour the city's Academy Museum to view a great statue of a young nude man

An interior view of the tomb of Lorenzo de' Medici, one of Florence's most famous Renaissance rulers. Michelangelo was responsible for many of the sculptures included in the design of the tomb.

carrying a slingshot. The marble statue, nearly 17 feet tall, depicts the biblical hero David. The figure is captured in stone at the moment he is preparing to do battle with the great Philistine soldier-giant, Goliath. Before their art tour of Florence is complete, these same visitors might pay a call to the Medici [MEH dee chee] Chapel of San Lorenzo, to admire the tomb of Lorenzo de' Medici, one of Florence's most famous Renaissance rulers.

In the Italian capital of Rome, visitors can enjoy other important Renaissance works of art. In the Vatican, where the leader of the Roman Catholic Church, the pope, lives, visitors can go to St. Peter's Church and stare in quiet reverence at the *Pieta*, a statue of the Virgin Mary and her son Jesus, lying dead across her lap, having just been taken down from the cross. At the nearby Sistine Chapel, visitors might crane their necks to take in several thousand square feet of paintings that adorn the chapel's ceiling, several stories above. The murals include hundreds of colorfully painted human figures from the pages of the Bible, including Adam and Eve, Noah, and the Hebrew prophets. Visitors might also admire a large painting on the chapel's altar wall, depicting the Last Judgment. Elsewhere in the complex of church art at St. Peter's, visitors can view a monumental marble sculpture of Moses, the Hebrew leader of the Exodus.

These noted works of Renaissance art—the marble statues of Moses, David, and the slain Christ, and the paintings in the Sistine Chapel—all rank as some of the most important and greatest works of art produced during the 1400s and 1500s. No trip to Italy would be complete without viewing each work on its own merit. Each is extraordinary as a single work of art, but each work also represents part of the talented genius of the Renaissance artist and sculptor we know as Michelangelo.

In a world of great and talented men, this single sculptor and painter towers above nearly all others, with only a few exceptions among his fellow artists— the older Leonardo da Vinci and the younger Raphael, to name two. Michelangelo proved to be one of the most significant figures of the Renaissance period. One can only wonder how one man could produce so many works of art during one of the most productive and creative periods for painting and sculpture.

He was, for one thing, an extremely versatile man, able to express himself in many different ways. He was not only an accomplished painter and sculptor, but also an architect who designed some of the most important buildings in Rome. He was a poet who wrote more than 300 works of verse. In addition, he wrote more than 500 letters that are still in existence today.

This nineteenth-century portrait of Michelangelo Buonarroti provides a glimpse of the esteemed sculptor and painter of the Italian Renaissance.

Michelangelo's success during the Renaissance was about more than talent and nurturing a variety of different interests. He was also a man driven by passion. He wanted to achieve, in his art, models of beauty—artwork that would fill the viewer with awe and an appreciation for his sense of dramatic style. The Renaissance was a time during which men and women sought new ways to express themselves. It was a time when a man with the gift of creativity could become a great and important person. Michelangelo could not have been born at a better time. For more than 60 years, this amazing artist drove himself to create. With that driving passion, he managed not only to create great works of art, but also to define an entire age of artistic expression.

Test Your Knowledge

1 Michelangelo was the artist and sculptor
responsible for which work(s) of art?
   a. The Sistine Chapel
   b. The statue of David
   c. The *Pieta*
   d. All of the above

2 In addition to his work as a sculptor and artist,
in what other field did Michelangelo excel?
   a. Poetry
   b. Engineering
   c. Astronomy
   d. Cooking

3 What was Lorenzo de' Medici of Florence
known for?
   a. He was an artist.
   b. He was a famous ruler of Florence during
      the Renaissance.
   c. He had St. Peter's Church built.
   d. He lived in Florence but was buried
      elsewhere.

4 In what museum is the statue of David housed?
   a. The Academy Museum
   b. The Uffizi Museum
   c. The Medici Museum
   d. The National Museum

5 Why is this period of time called the Renaissance?

a. All art was drawn in a new way.

b. It was a time of "rebirth" for the arts and sciences.

c. The Catholic Church paid for all the artwork being created.

d. It is named for an Italian style of art.

ANSWERS: 1. d; 2. a; 3. b; 4. a; 5. b

The Artist's Youth

Michelangelo, perhaps the greatest artist of the Italian Renaissance, was born on March 6, 1475. The son of the local governor of the tiny village of Caprese, nestled in the Apennine Mountains of Tuscany, he was baptized as Michelagnolo di Lodovico Buonarroti Simoni. In English, the spelling became "Michelangelo."

The Buonarroti Simoni family had been wealthy once. Michelangelo's great-grandfather had been a rich and successful banker. His grandfather, also a banker, had not fared as well, however. His father, Lodovico Buonarroti, as the mayor of Caprese, could hardly be called successful or wealthy. Although his family descended from the rich and famous among Italy's important families, Lodovico Buonarroti, his wife, Francesca, and young Michelangelo lived very modestly. The mayorship of Caprese paid very little, but hard work was something only the poor had to do. Lodovico Buonarroti was a proud man who would rather accept a meager income as a small-time government official than do work with his hands. Little did he realize that one day his new infant son would become famous for using his hands to create great works of art.

Within a month of Michelangelo's birth, Lodovico Buonarroti packed up his family and their belongings and moved to Florence. The Buonarrotis lived in an old house near the Church of Santa Croce. In the late fifteenth century, Florence was one of the most important city-states in Italy. Others included the cities of Venice, Rome, and Milan. Florence was already famous for two things—its woolens trade and its fabulous art. Although Michelangelo was only a baby, he also had a brother who was less than a year and a half older. While little is known of Michelangelo's upbringing, it is clear that his mother was often sick. Between 1475 and 1481, Francesca Buonarroti gave birth not only to Michelangelo, but also to three more sons. Due to his wife's poor condition and her nearly constant pregnancies, Lodovico Buonarroti turned Michelangelo over to the wife of a stonecutter who helped raise the young boy. (One story claims that Francesca Buonarroti had fallen from a horse during the early months of her pregnancy with Michelangelo and was unable to nurse her infant son.)

The Buonarrotis did not have much money, but they did own a small farm in the village of Settignano, in the hills overlooking Florence. It was there that the stonecutter and his wife lived. During Michelangelo's early years, the village of Settignano served as his home. The young Buonarroti also frequently visited the local stone quarries, places where workers cut stone for buildings, roads, and making statues. Some of Michelangelo's earliest memories were about stone.

Despite a lack of information about Michelangelo's early years, we do know that his mother died when he was only six years old. How much time the

The Renaissance: A New Vision for the World of Art

As a future artist, young Michelangelo could not have lived during a better time than the end of the fifteenth and the beginning of the sixteenth centuries. His life overlapped one of the greatest artistic periods in European history, the Renaissance.

The Renaissance was a dramatic period of growth and change in the world of art, as well as other fields of study and culture. It lasted for two centuries, from approximately 1400 A.D. to 1600. This important era in Europe came at the end of the Middle Ages, a time period that began when the old Roman Empire collapsed, around the year 400 A.D.

The word *renaissance* comes from an Italian word, *rinascimento*, which means "revival" or "rebirth." For modern historians, the Renaissance represents a rebirth in learning, in the study of true science and astronomy, and a significant change in the subject matter portrayed by painters and sculptors.

Italy was the center of the Renaissance. Its scholars and great minds, as well as its artists, admired the

young boy had spent with her, or even how he felt about losing her, remains unknown. It is known that young Michelangelo, once he came home to live in

earlier cultures of the Greeks and the Romans. They sought to return to many of the values held by these earlier societies, including their philosophy, writings, and art.

Just as Greek philosophers had placed tremendous importance on the individual and on natural beauty, so did Renaissance artists. Much of the art of the Middle Ages had focused on portraying stories from the Bible and Christian subjects. While Renaissance artists still painted and sculpted biblical subjects, they were more free to express themselves through their art. Their subjects were more emotional, more sensual, and more realistic. Painting or sculpting a nude subject had been avoided during the Middle Ages, but Renaissance artists, such as Michelangelo, thought it was important to show the beauty of the human body. The result was an artistic heritage that is still admired today.

his father's house permanently, shared the household with many family members. There were his four brothers and his father, of course. In addition, an aunt and uncle also lived in the Buonarroti house, along with Michelangelo's grandmother, his father's mother.

EARLY EDUCATION

How much Lodovico Buonarroti contributed to his son's upbringing is not clear. In his later years, Michelangelo described his father as "an old-fashioned man, who feared God." [1] While he provided the basics for a large family, he was "too proud to work for a living, too poor to live well." [2] Like many Italian fathers of that time, Michelangelo's father probably left much of his son's teaching to other family members. Lodovico Buonarroti did, however, give the following advice to his son, in a letter: "If you fall sick, you are destroyed. Be sure to protect your head and keep it reasonably warm; and never wash! Have a massage if you like, but never wash!" [3]

Michelangelo's father did have plans for his son. Despite his limited funds, he sent Michelangelo to school in 1482, when the boy was only seven. By age

This bronze bust of Michelangelo shows what he might have looked like as an adult. Little is known, however, about Michelangelo's life as a young child.

ten, Michelangelo was attending Latin school, where he began his training as a gentleman. Lodovico Buonarroti intended for his son to become an important military leader or government figure. Perhaps he might become a Florentine banker like his great-grandfather, or a rich merchant.

In school, according to one of his later biographers, Michelangelo became well read and he wrote with flowing handwriting. He enjoyed writing poetry. In fact, poetry would always be an important part of Michelangelo's life, even as an adult. With such talents, his father thought Michelangelo might become a learned writer or philosopher. Whatever Michelangelo might become in life, there was one career his father did not want for him. Lodovico Buonarroti did not want his son to become an artist or a sculptor. Michelangelo's father did not like artists, and thought such work was beneath his son. To Lodovico Buonarroti, "art was considered a manual craft and a lowly occupation."[4]

While in school, however, young Michelangelo showed a unique talent for and interest in drawing. When his interest remained strong, his father tried to steer him into other interests. Nothing seemed to

While young Michelangelo was in school, he showed a unique talent for and interest in drawing. Years later, he would complete this drawing entitled *Head of a Young Woman*, showing his attention to the details of the human form.

work. Lodovico Buonarroti became desperate to turn Michelangelo away from the world of art. To discourage him from taking on art as his life's work, Michelangelo's father beat him several times, but such punishment could not keep the young man from continuing to dream of becoming a sculptor.

Test Your Knowledge

1 Michelangelo's father was employed as
  a. a banker.
  b. a stonecutter.
  c. a village mayor.
  d. a painter.

2 In what city was Michelangelo born?
  a. Florence
  b. Rome
  c. Venice
  d. Caprese

3 Which of the following careers did Michelangelo's father *not* want for his son?
  a. Military leader
  b. Artist
  c. Philosopher
  d. Government figure

4 In addition to art, for which of the following was Florence known?
  a. Its woolens trade
  b. Its rivers
  c. Its churches
  d. Its food

5 Michelangelo was one of how many children?
   a. Two
   b. Three
   c. Four
   d. Five

ANSWERS: 1. c; 2. d; 3. b; 4. a; 5. d

Learning
His Craft

Finally, when his son was 13, Lodovico Buonarroti gave in. Michelangelo was turned over to a local artist, a painter named Domenico Ghirlandaio, to learn. The apprenticeship began on April 1, 1488. Ghirlandaio was extremely well known in Florence. He ran an art school where he taught other young men the arts of

21

painting and sculpting. Although only 13, Michelangelo arrived in Ghirlandaio's workshop three years later than was customary. Most boys began their apprenticeship to artists by age ten.

While under Ghirlandaio's direction, Michelangelo learned the skills an artist needed. He studied fresco painting, a type of painting done on wet plaster that allowed the paint to absorb into the plaster, keeping the colors bright. This style of painting was extremely popular during the Italian Renaissance. Young Michelangelo's apprenticeship was supposed to last for three years, but the student from Tuscany remained under Ghirlandaio's instruction for only one year. Years later, when he wrote his life story, Michelangelo claimed that he had not learned much from Ghirlandaio. He would, however, one day put to good use the skill of fresco painting, when he was hired to paint the ceiling of an important chapel.

Ghirlandaio may also have introduced Michelangelo to another form of art—sculpture. The accomplished master had a strong admiration for early Greek and Roman sculpture. Michelangelo also became an inspired admirer of such ancient stone carvings and sculpture. In fact, the young budding artist became convinced that painting was not one of the nobler art forms. To Michelangelo, sculpture had no equal in the art world. By 1489, the young artist left Ghirlandaio's workshop to take up his studies in the studio of a noted sculptor named Giovanni di Bertoldo.

Bertoldo was an old man when Michelangelo arrived in his studio, but he had studied under Donatello, one of the great Renaissance sculptors. The move to Bertoldo's workshop was an important step for young Michelangelo. His new sculpting teacher was the director of one of the greatest collections of ancient Roman sculpture in Italy. It was owned by the ruler of Florence, Lorenzo de' Medici, a powerful and influential man in both politics and the art world. Michelangelo was allowed to visit Lorenzo de' Medici's collection, which was located in the gardens of San Marco.

Under Bertoldo's direction, Michelangelo became a skilled sculptor. His talent was so obvious to his fellow students, some of them became jealous of him. One student, a young man named Pietro Torrigiano, became Michelangelo's rival. On one occasion, Torrigiano became so angry at Michelangelo, he struck him with his fist. The story was later included in *The Lives of the Painters*, a famous book written during the Renaissance by an artist named Vasari. In the story, Torrigiano explained what happened:

> This Buonarroti and I used to go along together when we were boys to study in Masaccio's [a famous early Renaissance painter] chapel in the church of the Carmine. Buonarroti had the habit of making fun of anyone else who was drawing there, and one day he provoked me so much that I lost my temper more than usual, and, clenching my fist, gave him such a punch on the nose that I felt the bone and cartilage crush like a biscuit. So that fellow will carry my signature till he dies.[5]

Torrigiano was correct. For the rest of his life, Michelangelo's most distinct facial feature would be his misshapen, flattened nose.

IN THE HOUSE OF THE MEDICIS

Michelangelo's talent at sculpting did not pass unnoticed by Lorenzo de' Medici. In 1590, Medici commissioned sculptures to be placed inside the vast Medici family library, which housed one of the greatest collections of manuscripts and books from the ancient world. Wanting to make a contribution to the collection, young Michelangelo borrowed a piece of marble from the library workers and began chiseling a sculpture of an aged faun, a mythical creature with a man's head and a goat's horns and ears. The young artist copied his faun from a battered and broken ancient faun sculpture. When Lorenzo de' Medici saw the finished work, "he marveled exceedingly . . . and praised the workmanship."[6]

On that occasion, Lorenzo de' Medici also joked with Michelangelo, telling the artist he had made a mistake by sculpting the old faun with a full set of teeth. Because Michelangelo was an extremely serious student, he waited until Medici left, then took his chisel and removed one of the faun's teeth. He even drilled holes in the gums where the tooth's roots would have been. Later, when the Florentine ruler saw the change Michelangelo had made, he was both amused and impressed. "Seeing the willingness and single-mindedness of the child . . . he thought to bestow his favor upon such a genius and take him into his house."[7] Soon, 15-year-old art student Michelangelo was living in Lorenzo de' Medici's palace. As for this early sculpture of Michelangelo's, the whereabouts of the faun is unknown.

Within the lavish palace of Lorenzo de' Medici, young Michelangelo was allowed to eat at the table of the Florentine ruler, along with his teacher, Bertoldo. (Bertoldo, however, would die in 1491.) Living in the Medici court, Michelangelo came into contact with some of Florence's most famous people, including other artists, painters, sculptors, and poets. He met several of the Medici family's children, including Giovanni, who later became Pope Leo X. Although he was only a teenager at the time, Giovanni de' Medici had already been appointed to the important church office of cardinal. Michelangelo also met Giuliano de' Medici. Decades later, after Michelangelo had become a famous sculptor, he would design a series of tombs where Giuliano de' Medici would be buried.

Here, within the household of the ruling family of Florence, Michelangelo had access to wealth and luxury. Art was everywhere within the Medici family complex. There were paintings and sculpture, as well as decorative works. Lorenzo de' Medici had one of the largest and grandest collections of ancient works, including coins, medallions, carved ivory cameos, and jewelry. One of the poets living in the palace, Angelo Poliziano, became a close friend and tutor to Michelangelo, one who "spurred him on in his studies, always explaining things to him and giving him subjects."[8]

By his late teens, Michelangelo was determined to make sculpting his life's work. Between 1491 and 1492, he produced one of his earliest works that is still known today, *The Battle of the Centaurs*. The small work, sculpted in marble, featured some two dozen nude Greek men and mythical centaurs fighting one another in a pitched battle. Already, Michelangelo's sculpture was mirroring his fascination with the human body. The work was completed just before Lorenzo de' Medici died in 1492.

NEW OPPORTUNITIES

After Lorenzo de' Medici's death, Michelangelo's life changed directions. While the Florentine ruler had been a strong figure, his son Piero was not. In

After the death of Lorenzo de' Medici (shown here), Michelangelo's life changed direction. He went with the exiled Medici family to live in Bologna, Italy.

fact, Piero de' Medici fell from power within a matter of months. When the Medici family was driven from Florence into exile, in 1494, Michelangelo decided to go with them to live in Bologna, another Italian city-state. He stayed for about a year, in the house of a nobleman, a friend of the Medicis'. For the time being, Florence was no longer the center of Michelangelo's life, but his study of sculpting and of the human body continued. He was hired to sculpt three marble figures in Bologna. He constantly searched for new ways to learn more about the human form. Michelangelo even visited the Hospital of Santo Spirito, where he was allowed to cut open human corpses to find out how specific muscles were shaped. In Bologna, things went well for the young Michelangelo, who was approaching 20 years of age.

By late 1495, despite his comfortable living conditions and sculpting work in Bologna, Michelangelo decided to return to Florence. He moved back into his father's household. Although the young sculptor was home, Florence was no longer a comfortable place for an artist such as Michelangelo. A popular monk named Savonarola was preaching in the

Florence During the Renaissance

By the 1400s, Europe was being redefined by its urban centers. Many of these important cities were located in Italy, including Venice, Milan, and its neighbor to the south, Florence. Florence's wealth was based on extensive banking and manufacturing, such as the woolens industry. In fact, by the 1400s, one out of every three Florentines was involved in the woolens trade, but this city of some 100,000 people would also serve as the model city of Renaissance art.

It was the first great city of the Renaissance. Even before Michelangelo was born, such early Renaissance artists as the sculptors Ghiberti and Donatello, the painter Masaccio, and the architect Brunelleschi, had creatively established the style of a period that Michelangelo built on in all three art forms—sculpting, painting, and architecture.

During Michelangelo's long career in Florence, he produced great art in Florence alongside such masters as Leonardo da Vinci and Raphael. Such artists would have been unable to produce the number of quality art works in Florence or any other European city without financial support. One of the leading families that supported the arts in Florence was the Medici family. They greatly influenced the Renaissance in Italy and France until the 1700s.

The Medici family was wealthy. Much of their wealth came from banking. They used this economic power to take political power in cities such as Florence, taking power in that city in 1434. Throughout most of the 1400s, banker Cosimo de' Medici and his grandson Lorenzo the Magnificent controlled power and politics in Florence. They also controlled its art.

In 1444, Cosimo de' Medici ordered the building of the first of the Medici palaces, called the Palazzo Medici. He also established the first public library in Europe since the collapse of the old Roman Empire. His collection of literary works was extensive, the result of Cosimo de' Medici spending what would be equivalent to millions of dollars on rare manuscripts and books.

It was Medici support of a talented group of painters and sculptors, however, that helped to establish Florence as the single most important art capital of Renaissance Europe. The list of artists they supported includes the best and most creative men of their age, such as Donatello, Filippino Lippi, Masaccio, Verrocchio, Botticelli, Ghirlandaio, Da Vinci, and, of course, Michelangelo.

streets of the city against popular art. Savonarola believed that much of Italian Renaissance art was indecent and extremely worldly. He believed that all art should be about religion. Michelangelo decided he could not remain in Florence. With the help of the Medicis, he made plans to go to Rome, another important Italian city-state and art center.

Rome was the center of life for many people living in northern Italy. It was also the religious center of the Roman Catholic Church. The pope lived there in a church complex called the Vatican. Many important Renaissance art projects were created in Rome, especially at the request of a pope or other important church leaders. For Michelangelo, Rome represented both an opportunity and a limitation for his art. As a freethinking young man, he did not especially like religious art. It was not important to him that art encourage someone to become more religious. Michelangelo once said that such art was only good "for women, especially old or very young women, as well as for monks, nuns and certain aristocrats."[9] He believed that when he created a sculpture in the form of the human body, he was closer to God.

ARRIVAL IN ROME

When Michelangelo arrived in Rome, as a young man of 22, he carried letters from the Medicis. The young artist was introduced to Cardinal Raffaele Riario, one of Rome's most powerful and wealthy members of the clergy. Similar to Lorenzo de' Medici, the cardinal was also a collector of ancient Roman sculpture. Michelangelo said the collection included "many beautiful things." [10]

When he learned that Michelangelo was a sculptor, Cardinal Riario gave him a large block of marble and told him to "show what he could do." [11] Michelangelo wrote about the offer in a letter to his former patron, Lorenzo de' Medici, on July 2, 1496. Of the cardinal's reactions, after showing the young Florentine artist his collection of old Roman statues, he wrote:

> [He] asked me whether I had courage enough to attempt some work of art of my own. I replied that I could not do anything as fine, but that he should see what I could do. We have bought a piece of marble for a life-sized figure and on Monday I shall begin work. [12]

Michelangelo had not even been in Rome a week before receiving his first important offer to sculpt. Ready to prove himself, he set out to carve his largest sculpture to date, a larger-than-life statue of the mythical Roman god Bacchus, the god of wine. Michelangelo had chosen to carve a figure that was hardly a religious one. His work on the statue took over a year to complete. Michelangelo, in fact, may not have finished the sculpture until 1498. He may also have worked on other statues, but it appears he either did not finish them or, perhaps, bought other marble blocks, but never even began work on them. When he finally finished his statue of Bacchus, he showed the work to Cardinal Riario. Unfortunately the cardinal was not happy with the statue. Apparently the cardinal's challenge to Michelangelo had never been important, as the cardinal was only interested in ancient Roman statues, not modern ones.

The work Michelangelo had poured into his sculpture *was* appreciated by someone else, however. His Bacchus statue was purchased by Jacopo Galli, a Roman banker who had a garden of ancient Roman sculpture, just as Cardinal Riario had. Michelangelo's meeting with Galli also proved

Shortly after arriving in Rome, Michelangelo received his first important offer to sculpt. He would carve his largest sculpture to date, a larger-than-life statue of the mythical Roman god Bacchus, the god of wine.

important for what came next in the young artist's career. Through Galli, Michelangelo was introduced to Jean Villiers de Fezenzac, a French cardinal. The cardinal wanted a religious statue carved. He asked Michelangelo to chisel a marble statue of the Virgin Mary holding the body of her son Jesus, after his death on the cross. The banker Galli probably worked out the deal for an anxious Michelangelo.

The contract was signed on August 27, 1498. Michelangelo was to complete the sculpture within one year and he would be paid 450 ducats. The statue was to be placed in a public location inside the Church of St. Peter's in Rome. Galli expressed great confidence in his young sculptor friend. He wrote that the planned statue, known as the *Pieta,* would one day be "the most beautiful work of marble in Rome, one that no living artist could better." [13] Galli could not have known at the time how right his prediction would prove to be.

Test Your Knowledge

1 Michelangelo began his apprenticeship in the arts at what age?

a. 10

b. 13

c. 12

d. 15

2 What is a fresco?

a. A painting on wet plaster

b. A type of sculpture

c. A painting on stone

d. A type of canvas

3 Michelangelo's rival Pietro Torrigiano once became so enraged at the young artist that he

a. destroyed his sculptures.

b. burned his drawings.

c. punched him in the nose.

d. had him expelled from school.

4 Lorenzo de' Medici first noticed Michelangelo's talent from the artist's sculpture of

a. a faun.

b. a lion.

c. a goat.

d. a soldier.

5 To learn more about the human form, Michelangelo
visited

a. an art school.

b. a hospital.

c. the Olympic Games.

d. a gymnasium.

The Heart
of a Sculptor

By late August 1498, Michelangelo was already under contract to sculpt a monumental work of art. The contract was clear and straightforward. It identified the statue Michelangelo was to complete as the *Pieta*. It defined the subject as "a Virgin Mary clothed, with the dead Christ in her arms, of the size of a proper man." [14]

The artist was to be paid in gold ducats from the Vatican mint, and the clock was ticking on the project. Michelangelo had one year to work. The work was probably intended to mark the cardinal's future burial site.

Michelangelo had already begun laying the ground work for the project, even before the documents were signed. The young artist had already visited the famous marble quarries at Carrara, in his native Tuscany. These previous trips to Carrara were probably his first to the quarries. Over the years that followed, he was a regular visitor at the marble pits. He became close friends with many of the quarry workers and masons. Sometimes he would stay at the Carrara quarries for months at a time, scouting for just the right blocks of marble that he would one day fashion into famous works of art. As for the proper marble block for his *Pieta*, he selected one that was wider than it was tall. His Virgin Mary, after all, would be seated holding Christ on her lap.

With the *Pieta* project assigned to him, Michelangelo established a workshop and hired a staff of artists. Michelangelo's *Pieta* was not the first one created during the Renaissance. Earlier examples already

The *Pieta,* one of Michelangelo's monumental works of art, showed the Virgin Mary with Christ dead in her arms.

existed, but they had been created by artists of the Northern Renaissance, not by Italians. Most early versions had included St. John the Baptist and

Mary Magdalene, a woman who had been a follower of Christ. Michelangelo, however, was only interested in creating a grand sculpture of the Virgin Mother and Jesus. Some art historians suspect that Michelangelo may have carved his *Pieta* with himself and his own mother in mind. She had died young, remember, when he was just six years old. Art historians have noted that Michelangelo chiseled his Virgin Mary to look quite young, perhaps the age his mother had been when she died.

The fact that Michelangelo's Virgin Mary looked so young caused some to criticize him. According to one source, Michelangelo explained why he carved Mary in her youth:

> I would say to you that such freshness and flower of youth, besides being preserved in her in so natural a way, has also possibly been helped by divine means in order to prove to the world the virginity and . . . purity of the Mother. . . . Therefore you should not be surprised if . . . I made the holy Virgin Mother of God much younger, in comparison with her Son, than her age would normally require.[15]

As Michelangelo set out to carve his *Pieta*, he wanted to create a work he described as "the heart's image." [16] He had in mind a highly emotional work. Mary would have Jesus stretched across her lap after being pulled from the cross. She would be young, even younger looking than Jesus himself. Her face would not show grief, but she would look content, as if accepting her son's sacrifice. To place Christ across Mary's lap and yet help keep Mary's face as the focus of the sculpture, Michelangelo had to make the Virgin larger than life—literally. Although Jesus lying down was the size of an adult man, Mary, if she could have stood up, would have been at least seven feet tall. Her size did not make the sculpture appear to be out of proportion, however. Michelangelo addressed this very thing when he wrote, "It is necessary to keep one's compass in one's eyes and not in the hand, for the hands execute, but the eye judges." [17] What one sees in Michelangelo's *Pieta* is not a Mary who is too tall, but the Mother of God who is quiet and comforting.

By the time Michelangelo finished his well-crafted work in stone, he had created a masterpiece. He had not been particularly famous before his

Pieta. He was only 24 when the work was completed, but, after creating the statue, his name would become famous across Italy and much of Europe. Despite his youth, he had already proven himself to be more talented than many of his older, fellow artists. Michelangelo, it seems, was an overnight success. Unfortunately Cardinal Villiers was unable to see the completed sculpture. He had died during the year Michelangelo was working on the *Pieta.*

The *Pieta* would be the only sculpture or work of art that Michelangelo would ever put his name to—literally. According to a story written in Vasari's account:

> One day coming into the place were [the *Pieta*] had been installed, Michelangelo found a large number of strangers from Lombardy praising it highly. One of them asked another who had made it, and he replied, "Our Gobbo from Milan." Michelangelo kept his counsel though it seemed rather strange to him that his painstaking work should be attributed to someone else. One night, bringing his chisels along, he locked himself in with a little light and carved his name there.[18]

When Michelangelo carved his name on the *Pieta*, he did so in an obvious place. On the sash that diagonally crossed the Virgin Mary's chest, the 24-year-old sculptor chiseled the following words: *MICHAELACELUS BONAROTUS FLOREN FACIEBA*. The translation: "Michelangelo Buonarroti the Florentine made this."

ANOTHER RETURN TO FLORENCE

In the two years that followed the completion of his *Pieta*, Michelangelo worked on several smaller, less significant projects. Galli, the banker, lined up a contract for Michelangelo to paint an altarpiece for a burial chapel of a bishop in St. Agostino, but the altarpiece was never finished. The uncompleted oil painting hangs today in London's National Gallery. Michelangelo did, within two years of finishing the *Pieta*, produce another statue of the Virgin Mary and Jesus, known as the *Bruges Madonna*. This time, however, Jesus was sculpted as an infant. The work was completed in 1501.

By then, Michelangelo was once again on the move. He had been in Rome for five years, had already fashioned a monumental sculpture, and

Jesus was the subject of several of Michelangelo's sculptures. This face of Christ, from a crucifix by Michelangelo, features Jesus as an adult, but Michelangelo's *Bruges Madonna* statue, completed in 1501, portrayed Jesus as an infant.

had become famous. Friends began urging him to return to Florence, the city of his roots. That spring, the fields of Tuscany were thick with flowers, and the orchards were fragrant with blossoms. As Michelangelo made his way to Florence, he felt as though he was returning to his homeland. In some of his writings, he called the city of his youth his "nest." [19]

In addition to being homesick for his family, Michelangelo was also interested in returning to Florence for another reason. According to Vasari, one of his biographers, the 26-year-old artist had received letters from some of his fellow Florentines

> telling him that, if he came back, he might have the big piece of marble that Piero Soderini, then *gonfaloniere* of the city, had talked of giving to Leonardo da Vinci, but was not proposing to present to Adrea Sansovino, an excellent sculptor, who was making every effort to get it.[20]

It was a block of marble Michelangelo was definitely interested in, weighing several tons and standing 18 feet high. It had been worked by another sculptor, Agostino di Duccio. In Vasari's words, "he had hacked a hole between the legs, and it was altogether misshapen and reduced to ruin."[21] The work had been so mishandled, it had been left unfinished. For 35 years, the block of marble had stood in the work yard of the local cathedral as "a ghostly reminder to all young sculptors of the challenge of their craft."[22]

Michelangelo's interest in the marble block everyone called "the Giant," may have begun 12 years earlier, when he saw the sculptures in Lorenzo de' Medici's palace gardens. When he reached Florence, one of the first things Michelangelo did was to appeal to the cathedral board to give him permission to work on the abandoned marble. The members of the board seemed interested in Michelangelo's request, familiar with his talent from his years in Rome, but their decision did not come immediately.

In the meantime, Michelangelo found work elsewhere. He took employment on a sculpting project in Siena. He had, in fact, contracted for the work earlier that spring just before he left Rome. He would decorate the family chapel of Cardinal Francesco Piccolomini. The chapel was connected to the cathedral in Siena. Michelangelo had begun work on a series of 15 statues of various saints, when he received word from the cathedral board. The "giant" block of marble was his. By that fall, he would begin to work on a sculpture that would become one of his greatest works.

Test Your Knowledge

1 The Vatican gave Michelangelo how long to complete the *Pieta*?

a. Six months

b. One year

c. Five years

d. Eighteen months

2 What did Michelangelo's *Pieta* depict?

a. John the Baptist and Mary Magdalene

b. The Pope

c. The Virgin Mother holding Jesus

d. Angels surrounding Christ

3 Michelangelo frequently visited stone quarries for what reason?

a. To select the best piece of marble

b. To plan his next sculpture

c. To recruit stonecutters as his assistants

d. To pray for inspiration

4 After leaving Rome in 1501, Michelangelo traveled to

a. Florence.

b. Venice.

c. Germany.

d. Spain.

5 What was "The Giant"?

   a. Michelangelo's most famous sculpture

   b. A block of marble left from another artist's unfinished sculpture

   c. A painting that inspired Michelangelo

   d. The nickname of one of Michelangelo's patrons

ANSWERS: 1. b; 2. c; 3. a; 4. a; 5. b

The Stonecutter and the Shepherd Boy

By mid-August 1501, Michelangelo had signed a contract to carve a statue from the large, mangled piece of marble. From the beginning, the subject to be carved from the marble was that of the biblical hero David. He had been a shepherd boy who eventually became king of the Hebrew people of Israel. Even before Michelangelo was accepted as the sculptor of choice, the official commission referred to the figure to be carved from the stone block as a "David." Michelangelo was to be paid six gold florins each month for two years while he created the massive sculpture.

Once he signed the appropriate documents, Michelangelo wasted little time in taking his chisel to the block. On September 9, "with a few blows of a hammer, Michelangelo knocked off a 'certain knot' that had been on the chest of the future figure."[23] Four days later, he rose at dawn and began serious work on the waiting block. Michelangelo also ordered that a great, wooden shed be built to house the marble. Now he would not have to worry much about the weather, and he would be able to protect his work. He kept the shed locked at all times.

The sixteenth century was a good time to be working as an artist or even living in Florence. There were new and fresh possibilities for artists in the city. Some things, however, had not changed. The city was still home to important banks, churches, artist groups, and artwork. Following the death of Lorenzo de' Medici, however, his palace had been stripped of its art and furnishings. The fiery monk Savonarola had, by 1498, been arrested, tried for heresy, hanged in the public square in Florence, and his body had been burned. Politically, the city was experiencing both good and bad. While French armies had menaced the city in previous years, the French king, Louis XII, was an ally to several Italian city-states, including Florence. As for city politics, there were calls for a more stable constitution and a new central assembly. Florence, now a republic, was extremely prosperous, and money for artists, painters, and sculptors was available for the taking. Michelangelo was not the only artist to return to the reinvented Florence. In 1500, Leonardo da Vinci came back from Milan to the city where he had created so many of his great works of art.

Because the marble block that Michelangelo was working on was already damaged, and the figure to be carved from it was so large, Michelangelo had to figure out how to approach his *David*. Some stories say that Michelangelo, once he had access to the great stone block, immediately grabbed a chisel and began carving away, "making the chips fly off violently as he struggled to set free the image he saw within."[24] He was more of a planner and a perfectionist than that, however. In fact, he made sketches of various poses for his shepherd boy, who was to be nude. He completed detailed drawings from various models he formed of the different parts of his figure, including limbs and hands.

Most important, Michelangelo had to determine whether a figure could actually be carved from the block, despite the previous work that had been done on it. Again Vasari described Michelangelo's approach, "Michelangelo measured it all anew, considering whether he might be able to carve a reasonable figure from that block."[25] The Florentine sculptor then made a model of his figure in wax.

As was the style of the day, Michelangelo would have drawn the face of his shepherd boy on the face of the marble block, before carving back from the stone's front to create a fully shaped human figure. This approach is described in the writings of another artist, Benvenuto Cellini, when he writes about how to carve a figure from marble:

The best method ever was used by the great Michelangelo; after having drawn the principal view on the block, one begins to remove the marble from this side as if one were working a relief and in this way, step by step, one brings to light the whole figure.[26]

Despite the large scale of the statue that Michelangelo intended to carve, he remained excited by the challenge of creating a serious work of art. He worked diligently on his statue and was not bothered by distractions. Stories recorded how Michelangelo worked with a furious energy, putting in many hours. He despised taking time out, even to sleep. Sometimes, when he slept, he kept his clothes on, not wanting to take time out to remove them and put them on the next morning.

COMPLETING A MASTERPIECE

Michelangelo wanted nothing to keep him from his work. He ate little and probably slept even less. His work habits were described by another artist:

He has always been extremely temperate in living, using food more because it was necessary than for any pleasure he took in it; especially when he was engaged upon some great work; for then he usually confined himself to a piece of bread, which he ate in the middle of his labor. . . . [He slept little] for sleep . . . rarely suits his constitution, since he continually suffers from pains in the head during slumber, and any excessive amount of sleep [upsets] his stomach. While he was in full vigor, he generally went to bed with his clothes on, even to the tall boots. . . . At certain seasons he kept his boots on for such a length of time, that when he drew them off the skin came away together with the leather, like that of . . . a snake [shedding its skin].[27]

The fact that Michelangelo denied himself such comforts as good food, time to sleep, and personal cleanliness had almost nothing to do with a lack of money. He was becoming one of the best-paid artists in all of Italy.

By early 1504, Michelangelo had largely completed his colossal statue. Members of a Florentine government committee visited the sculptor's work site and got their first full view of the new *David*.

Michelangelo's *David, a* full-scale model of the biblical hero, required a great deal of planning. Once he got started on it, Michelangelo put in many hours carving, rarely taking time out for sleep.

They voted to accept the finished work and to place it wherever Michelangelo wanted it to go. He selected the Palazzo della Signoria, the center of Florentine government.

By mid-May 1504, the city leaders of Florence ordered Michelangelo's *David* to be moved from the shelter that had been built over his marble three years earlier. The moving was difficult. Many workers were used to take the marble figure down the city's narrow and winding streets. One eye-witness described the difficulties as follows:

> They broke the wall above the gateway enough to let it pass. That night some stones were thrown at the Colossus with intent to harm it. Watch had to be kept at night; and it made way very slowly, bound as it was upright, suspended in the air with enormous beams and intricate machinery of ropes. It took four days to reach the Piazza. . . . More than 40 men were employed to make it go; and there were 14 rollers joined beneath it, which were changed from hand to hand.[28]

Fortunately, after a long and difficult moving process, the statue reached its new home. Although the move had taken several days, the distance covered was approximately half a mile.

No one knows why someone decided to throw rocks at Michelangelo's masterpiece. Perhaps it was the work of some misguided vandals. Some have

A Sculptor's Tools

Michelangelo was an extremely dedicated artist. He labored with his great piece of marble to create his statue of *David*, putting in long hours and endless days of backbreaking work. Working with marble took lots of patience and nerves of steel. One misdirected blow to a tool might cause damage to a marble block that could not be repaired. To create a statue the size of *David*—which stood 13 feet tall—would have required tens of thousands of blows with the tools of the sculpting trade.

Today almost no carving tools dating back to the Renaissance have survived, but such tools were probably little different from modern tools used to sculpt marble and other stone. The primary tool was one that rarely ever touched the marble itself—a wooden mallet or hammer. With this mallet, an artist like Michelangelo would have used three types of chisels, metal tools struck by the hammer against the marble to remove some of the

suggested the attack was an organized effort by former supporters of the Medici family, to protest a new symbol of the new republican government's power. Despite the attack, once the statue was set in its new home, Michelangelo probably then put the

surface and create a new surface, that of the sculpture itself.

Among Michelangelo's chiseling arsenal, he would have used pointed chisels, toothed chisels, and smooth chisels. The pointed chisels would have been used first to chip away the outer stone. Then the artist would have used his toothed chisels to add detail to the sculpture. Finally he would have taken his smooth, flat chisels to create the smaller details on the statue.

While the hammer was used on all three types of chisels, it was not used with the final set of tools. In addition to chisels, the sculptor would have used hand-held rasps and files to create rounded edges and further definition. Some of that work, like that of the flat chisels, was among the most delicate. While strength and talent were the keys to beginning a great stone work of art, it was in the details that the artist often proved just how much talent he had.

At 13 feet tall, Michelangelo's *David* was larger than life. This sculpture also brought a larger-than-life image to Michelangelo as an artist.

finishing touches on his *David*. He probably gave the statue its final polishing, helping to create the shiny surface of the "skin." By early September, it was time to reveal the work of art that Michelangelo had labored over for three years. September 8 was the unveiling. When the people of Florence saw the completed work for the first time, they were awestruck. Everyone already knew the name Michelangelo. After his *David* was completed, however, he was thought of as the greatest of all Italian sculptors, and would be thought so for the rest of his life.

One of the important results of Michelangelo's work on his *David* was the fact that it marked a growth in his development as an artist. He had created a large, 13-foot-tall statue out of an abandoned and damaged piece of marble. His sculpture was larger than life. Perhaps Vasari best summed it all up when he said, "Truly it was a miracle on the part of Michelangelo to restore to life a thing that was dead."[29] In the same way, Michelangelo had re-created himself as a sculptor. He had emerged from the experience, as an artist, equally larger than life.

Test Your Knowledge

1 What was Michelangelo paid for sculpting his statue of David?

   a. Twelve pounds of silver

   b. Free room and board

   c. Six gold florins per month

   d. Free marble for his next work

2 What was Michelangelo's greatest challenge in creating his statue of David?

   a. Public opinion was against him.

   b. The stone was brittle.

   c. There was too little marble to work with.

   d. The marble was badly damaged.

3 To help him visualize the completed statue of David, Michelangelo

   a. consulted other sculptors.

   b. created a wax sculpture of David.

   c. completed a series of paintings.

   d. asked for more money.

4 What endangered the statue of David as it was moved to the Palazzo della Signoria?

   a. Rock-throwing vandals

   b. Narrow clearances and low archways

   c. The chance that the ropes supporting it would break

   d. All of the above

5 Completion of Michelangelo's *David* caused which
   of the following?
   a. It put a strain on Michelangelo's health.
   b. It bankrupted Italy.
   c. It assured Michelangelo's place among Italy's
      best artists.
   d. It was met with public outrage.

ANSWERS: 1. c; 2. d; 3. b; 4. d; 5. c

The Pope and the Artist

The unveiling of Michelangelo's *David* was the crowning success for a career that was quickly becoming legendary. His reputation as an artist, especially as a sculptor, was firmly established. Patrons of the arts would flock to him, and, for the rest of his life, he would always be working. Well-paying commissions were routine and offers came from everywhere.

Even as he had labored on his *David*, Michelangelo was busy with other art projects. It was probably in his restless nature to move from one project to the next, even before he had completed the first. For the great Florentine sculptor, the years that opened the sixteenth century were extremely busy. Between 1500 and 1508, Michelangelo worked with a high-speed outpouring of talent. During those eight years, he accepted 18 offers to produce various works of art, from sculpture to painting. Some were very small and limited, such as producing a bronze dagger. Others were even more gigantic than his *David*. One of his biographers stated that Michelangelo even thought about accepting an offer to work as an architect for the sultan of Turkey. Apparently the sultan wanted someone to build a bridge from the city of Constantinople across the nearby body of water called the Bosporus. During these years, Michelangelo seemed incapable of turning down work.

There was seemingly no end to his productivity. In the first eight years of the 1500s, Michelangelo not only carved his giant *David* and the *Bruges*

Madonna, he also chiseled seven other sculptures, including a figure of St. Matthew, four smaller statues for an altar, and a pair of marble *tondi.* (A *tondi* was a round work of art.) In addition, he produced three works cast in bronze, including a copy of his *David,* which he sent to France, and a seated statue of Pope Julius II. Pope Julius would become one of Michelangelo's most important patrons during the last half of this productive eight-year period.

While most of the work Michelangelo completed during these years was sculpture, he also accepted commissions to paint. One work, painted in 1504, the same year his *David* was finished, was the *Doni Tondo* (*Holy Family*), a round painting measuring nearly four feet in diameter. The work was paid for by Florentine businessman Agnolo Doni. The work featured the Virgin Mary and the Christ Child, along with St. Joseph. The work also featured vivid colors—deep blues, dark greens, and orange-gold—and revealed Michelangelo's talent as a painter.

While Michelangelo was indeed a talented painter, he never really enjoyed or even appreciated the medium. He spoke and wrote about painting as a waste of time. He stated that oil painting was only "suitable for women . . . or for idlers."[30] As for painting landscapes, Michelangelo wrote that such works should be forbidden. He called them nothing but "a vague and deceitful sketch, a game for children and uneducated men."[31] Michelangelo believed that, as an art form, painting was vastly inferior to sculpture. In one writing, he stated, "The more painting resembles sculpture, the better I like it, and the more sculpture resembles painting, the worse I like it."[32] These were the words of a man who would soon begin work on one of the largest, grandest series of paintings produced during the High Renaissance.

ENTER POPE JULIUS II

With so many important works of art, Michelangelo was also being paid by some of the most important people in Italy. In Florence alone, he was hired as an artist by the head of the Florentine government, four wealthy and powerful families in Florence, the Cathedral of Florence, a French cardinal, the French finance minister, and a guild of rich merchants from northern France. Among those who employed Michelangelo for his artistic talents, none was more important or powerful than Pope Julius II.

Julius II had, only months earlier, been Cardinal Giuliano della Rovere. He had succeeded Pope Pius III, whose reign had lasted less than one month. Pope Julius II was the nephew of Pope Sixtus IV, who had ordered the construction of a chapel more than 30 years earlier, which was named for him— the Sistine Chapel. Like other popes of the 1400s and 1500s, Pope Julius was not only a religious leader, he commanded armies as well. He spent years of his papacy fighting to drive French armies from Italy, marching under the war cry, "Out with the Barbarians!"[33] His was a never-ending campaign. At one point during his reign, he vowed he would not shave his face again until the last of the French armies were gone from Italian soil. When he died in 1513, his beard was long and gray.

Michelangelo's reputation could not have escaped Pope Julius II's attention. The pope's chief architect in 1505 was a Florentine named Giuliano da Sangallo, a friend of Michelangelo's. It was Sangallo who suggested his fellow Florentine might be able to create great works of art for Pope Julius. That

March, the pope commanded Michelangelo to travel to Rome. The move away from Florence, where the sculptor of *David* and the *Pieta* had established his career, would be both a blessing and a curse for Michelangelo.

To be sure, Michelangelo could not have been called by a more dedicated patron of the arts than Pope Julius II. For years, Pope Julius had been a collector of ancient Roman sculpture, and he had quite a collection. The pope wanted to make Rome the center of the Renaissance. Up to that time, Florence had been considered the most important Italian city for art. Pope Julius dreamed of great art, sculpture, and architecture. He began calling the greatest artists in Europe to Rome, to decorate the existing churches, chapels, and papal buildings. The pope also wanted new buildings constructed, including a new Church of St. Peter's.

A TOMB FOR A POPE

He was a new pope, however, having been placed in power by one of the strong rulers in Italy, Cesare Borgia, late in 1503. Pope Julius would reign over the Catholic Church for nearly ten years. During

Pope Julius II wanted to make Rome the center of the Italian Renaissance. He wanted new buildings to be constructed, including St. Peter's Basilica. The nave of the famous church is shown here.

nearly all his years on the papal throne, Michelangelo was in Rome, working on the pope's elaborate art projects. When Michelangelo first arrived in Rome, Pope Julius had no specific plans or commissions for him. He simply wanted the Florentine sculptor to be "on hand and ready for use."[34] After a while, however, the pope set his sights on a monumental project equal to the talents of Michelangelo. The artist would design and construct the tomb where Pope Julius would be buried upon his death. One of Michelangelo's biographers described what happened next:

> At last it occurred to him to use his genius to construct his own tomb. The design furnished by Michelangelo pleased the Pope so much that he sent him off immediately to Carrara [the marble quarries], with a commission to quarry as much marble as was needful.[35]

Michelangelo spent eight months climbing up and down the quarries, looking for the best pieces of marble. According to the biographer Condivi, "Michelangelo stayed in these mountains . . . with two workmen and his horse, and without any other provision except his food."[36] The plan for the tomb was so elaborate, it included 40 statues. When Michelangelo returned to Rome, he brought back so much marble, it "stirred amazement in the minds of most folk, but joy in the Pope's."[37] Although the scope of the tomb was gigantic and complicated,

This statue of Moses was one of the 40 statues intended to decorate the tomb of Pope Julius II.

Michelangelo believed he could complete it all within five years. He could not have been more wrong.

Pride and overconfidence had overtaken the great Florentine artist. In fact, Michelangelo had taken on a project so grand and so complicated, he could not possibly have ever finished it. The tomb of Julius II was designed to measure 36 feet long and 24 feet wide, with a height of 36 feet. It was to be carved entirely from marble and include places where the 40 larger-than-life statues would provide depth and decoration.

At the top of the tomb display, Michelangelo was supposed to carve two angels who supported a sar-cophagus, a burial box for Julius. The sarcophagus, however, was only for decoration. According to the complete plan, the tomb was to include a chapel, "in the midst of which was a marble chest, wherein the corpse of the Pope was . . . to be deposited."[38] If the project had been completed as planned, it would have been like nothing in the art world since the days of ancient Roman emperors, such as Augustus Caesar.

One of the many problems with constructing such a large, elaborate tomb was that there was no church in Rome big enough to hold the papal monument.

Pope Julius soon came up with a solution; he would order the building of a new and larger St. Peter's, with a massive and impressive *basilica*, a rounded assembly area in a church where the Mass was spoken, to house his personal monument.

The plan for a new St. Peter's called for skilled architects. Sangallo, Michelangelo's friend, was one of them. Another was Donato Bramante, one of the greatest Italian architects of the High Renaissance from northern Italy, where he had recently worked in Milan under the military dictator Lodovico Sforza. After Sforza's fall from power, Bramante had arrived in Rome, looking for a patron and for work. As with Michelangelo, Bramante had a widespread reputation, and Pope Julius II employed him as an architect to work on St. Peter's. This decision would cause Michelangelo many personal problems for years to come.

Bramante became interested in creating St. Peter's without the help of any other architects who might become rivals. He and Sangallo did not get along, and Bramante worked hard at pushing Sangallo off the project entirely and out of Rome completely. When Sangallo and Bramante showed two different plans for a new St. Peter's to Pope Julius, the Holy Father chose Bramante's design over that of his friend Sangallo. (Sangallo had been friends with Julius for years, back when he was a cardinal.) A humiliated Sangallo did not remain in Rome much longer. No sooner was Sangallo out of the picture, when Bramante began trying to push Michelangelo out, as well. The biographer Condivi explained at least one of the reasons Bramante did not want Michelangelo to work on Pope Julius's tomb in his planned St. Peter's renovation:

> For Bramante, as everyone knows, was much given to pleasure . . . . The salary he received from the Pope, though it was great, was not nearly enough for him, so that he tried to make more by constructing walls of inferior material . . . Bramante realized that Michelangelo would have discovered his mistakes, and so he tried to deprive him of . . . the influence which he had gained over the Pope.[39]

Regardless of whether Bramante was behind the effort to exclude Michelangelo or not, for some reason, Pope Julius began losing interest in his tomb

and began separating himself from Michelangelo.
When the Florentine tried one day to pay a visit to
Pope Julius, he was denied entry by a lowly servant,

Two Renaissance Giants as Rivals

Michelangelo's lifetime overlapped with the lives of many of the most important and talented artists of the Italian Renaissance. One of them, who today is considered perhaps the most talented man of this entire artistic era, was Leonardo da Vinci. While the two men spent their careers pursuing their individual projects as painters, sculptors, and architects, their paths did cross on one occasion.

While Michelangelo was still working on his *David*, he signed an agreement to produce a wall mural for the new grand council hall of the Palazzo della Signoria in Florence. He was not the only artist, however, to agree to decorate the great civic chamber. Leonardo da Vinci had already agreed to produce a mural for the hall, as well. Suddenly the two Renaissance giants were rivals.

Both were to paint scenes of different battles from Florence's past. Leonardo da Vinci was to paint the Battle of Anghiari and Michelangelo had selected the 1364 Battle of Cascina as his subject. Soon everyone in Florence was buzzing about the two competing artists. On one occasion, the two artists

offending Michelangelo deeply. After writing a short letter to Pope Julius—"I give you notice that from this time forward, if you want me, you must look for

happened to meet on the streets of the city and exchanged insults. Things seemed to be shaping up for a great artistic rivalry.

Unfortunately the planned murals never happened. Michelangelo did manage to begin painting his fresco, as did Leonardo da Vicini. Near its completion, however, da Vinci's mural met with disaster. Always willing to experiment with his art, the elder artist had used some type of varnish mixture with his paint, which caused his paint colors to blur and run together, ruining his mural. Michelangelo never finished his mural, either, having been called to Rome by Pope Julius to take up other, grander art projects.

Today the remains of those murals are all gone, and only the drawings created by both men remain. The drawings show the true skill and talent both men carried through the Renaissance. As one contemporary artist, Benvenuto Cellini, wrote, "So long as [the drawings] remained intact, they were the school of the world."*

* Robert Coughlan, *The World of Michelangelo, 1475–1564*. New York: Time Incorporated, 1966, p. 107

me elsewhere than at Rome"—Michelangelo packed up and returned to Florence.[40]

Pope Julius was furious. He sent word to Michelangelo to return immediately to Rome. The struggle between the two powerful men went on for several months. Pope Julius sent three separate papal messengers to Florence to demand Michelangelo leave Florence and make his way back to Rome. By the third contact, the pope was threatening war between Florence and Rome. Florentine ruler Piero Soderini called Michelangelo before him. He told Michelangelo, "You have tried a bout with the Pope on which the King of France would not have ventured. . . . We do not wish to go to war on your account. . . . Make up your mind to return."[41]

At first, when Michelangelo returned, he and Pope Julius were not on the best of terms. After all, according to Michelangelo, "I was forced, a rope around my neck, to go and ask his pardon."[42] Pope Julius was in the middle of a military campaign against two papal states, whose rulers did not accept his religious power over them. Michelangelo and Pope Julius met one another not in Rome, but in the city of Bologna, which Pope Julius had just captured.

Their first encounter was tense. Pope Julius was still angry at Michelangelo for ignoring his demands for three months, but when a bishop in the room tried to explain to Pope Julius that he should forgive the artist because "such men were ignorant creatures, worthless except for their art," Julius redirected his anger against the bishop and hit him with his papal staff.[43] As the offending bishop was driven from the room, everything between the two Italian strong men—the church leader and the artist—appeared to be forgiven and forgotten.

Despite commanding an army, Pope Julius still had time to offer the newly returned Michelangelo a new project. The pope was interested in a large bronze-cast statue of himself, which he wanted placed in St. Peter's Cathedral. Pope Julius wanted himself seated on a throne, but, even then, the statue was to be more than ten feet tall. The pope offered 1,000 ducats, and Michelangelo, wanting to please him, agreed. The year was 1506, and the bronze project would occupy Michelangelo for the next two years.

Test Your Knowledge

1 What did the painting *Doni Tondo* depict?

    a. A cathedral

    b. A bridge across the Bosporus River

    c. The Virgin Mary, Christ Child, and
       St. Joseph

    d. The likeness of a wealthy patron

2 Michelangelo once said that oil painting was

    a. his life's calling.

    b. a waste of time.

    c. a good way to earn a living.

    d. the highest form of art.

3 What work did Pope Julius II *first* commission
from Michelangelo?

    a. The pope's own tomb

    b. A bronze sculpture of himself

    c. A painting of Rome

    d. A statue of David

4 The original sarcophagus design featured which
of the following?

    a. Tons of marble

    b. Elaborate sculpting not seen since Classical
      Rome

    c. Two large angels

    d. All of the above

5 What did Pope Julius II threaten if Michelangelo did not return to Rome?

a. A war against Florence

b. To withhold the artist's pay

c. A ban on Michelangelo's sculptures

d. Destruction of the statue of David

ANSWERS: 1. c; 2. b; 3. a; 4. d; 5. a

The Great Ceiling Painter

Making the immense bronze statue of Pope Julius II presented problems for Michelangelo. For one, he remained in Bologna, a city he did not much like, to work on the project. In addition, he did not have a great deal of experience in bronze casting, despite having made a bronze of *David*, which he sent to France. The 1,000 ducats in payment were not enough, and the great artist was soon strapped for money to live on. He hired three assistants to help him, but only rented one room for the four of them to share. They even slept in the same bed. In time, Michelangelo fired one of them, and a second one voluntarily left the project.

In several letters, Michelangelo complained to family members that the project was a difficult one for him, saying "I'm busy with nothing but working day and night, and I have endured and am enduring such labor that if I had another such again I don't think my life would be long enough."[44] The Florentine sculptor did complete the bronze statue, however, by mid-February 1508.

A week later, the great, polished bronze statue, *Julius the Colossus*, was placed above the main doors of the cathedral in Bologna. Unfortunately, despite working for two years, Michelangelo's bronze statue did not last long. In 1511, when another Italian army took control of Bologna, they attacked the statue, pulling it down with ropes, and the immense bronze work fell to the floor in a crash.

The great work of Michelangelo was eventually sold as bronze scrap, which was melted down and

Pope Julius II commissioned Michelangelo to create a large bronze statue to be placed in St. Peter's Cathedral (shown here). The statue would depict Pope Julius sitting on a throne.

recast into cannons. With the project completed that February, Michelangelo was ready to leave Bologna and return to his native Florentine homeland. He believed his return to Florence might be permanent, but Pope Julius soon caught up with him. Back from his military campaigns, Pope Julius was ready for Michelangelo to work for him again. A letter arrived in either late March or early April

1508, in which Pope Julius summoned Michelangelo once again to Rome.

The great sculptor assumed that Pope Julius wanted him to begin again his work on his tomb. That was not the case, however. The pope had a new project in mind for Michelangelo. It did not involve sculpting, but painting. It appears that Pope Julius had begun, as early as 1506, to consider offering Michelangelo a commission to paint the ceiling of a Vatican chapel built by his uncle, Sixtus IV. At that time, several of the chapel's walls had already been decorated by other earlier, but great Renaissance artists, such as Perugino, Signorelli, Botticelli, and Michelangelo's old teaching master, Ghirlandaio. These artists had painted scenes from the life of Jesus and Moses, the Old Testament leader. The ceiling, however, had never been frescoed. When Michelangelo was called to decorate the ceiling, it was painted pale blue, with a scattering of golden stars.

TO PAINT A CEILING

When Michelangelo realized he was being called to Rome to paint, not sculpt, he did not want to go.

Pope Julius II commissioned Michelangelo to paint
the ceiling of the Sistine Chapel in Rome. At first,
Michelangelo was reluctant to pursue the project. By
the time he finished the project, his great fresco
scenes would include more than 340 figures.

He did not consider himself a painter. He tried to get out of it, stating "painting is not my art."[45] Michelangelo even suggested Raphael, another artist, a highly skilled and talented painter from Urbino, as a replacement. Raphael was a younger kinsman of Bramante's, but Pope Julius insisted, offering Michelangelo 15,000 gold ducats, a very good payment.

Because Michelangelo had little experience at painting, it does seem strange that Pope Julius would order him to paint such a large fresco in such an important Vatican building. The Sistine Chapel served as Pope Julius's favorite private chapel. The chapel was huge and tall. The distance from its marble mosaic floor to the highest portion of the ceiling was 68 feet, taller than a modern five-story building. The entire ceiling to be painted covered a space measuring nearly 6,000 square feet. It would be difficult, at best, to design such a gigantic painting and fill such a great space. In addition, the ceiling was not flat. It was a vaulted ceiling, meaning it was curved. Anyone painting on that surface would need to paint his figures so that the curvature of the ceiling did not distort or misshape them. Truly, the ceiling of the Sistine Chapel called for an artist of extraordinary talent.

Later in life, Michelangelo became convinced that Bramante was the reason behind Pope Julius's insistence that Michelangelo paint the ceiling. In Michelangelo's mind, Bramante did not want Michelangelo's work on Pope Julius's unfinished tomb to take money away from his rebuilding of St. Peter's. (Pope Julius's military campaigns had put a strain on the Vatican treasury.) Michelangelo believed Bramante was sure that the project would prove too big for Michelangelo and would cause him to fail. This would lower Michelangelo's standing in the eyes of Pope Julius, leaving Bramante as the only artist and architect who could be trusted and relied upon. There is little proof, however, that Bramante schemed against Michelangelo by setting him up to fail at painting the Sistine Chapel ceiling.

Originally, Pope Julius's plan for the ceiling was for Michelangelo to paint the Twelve Apostles, but Michelangelo, once he was committed to the project, rejected that idea. "That will be a poor effort, Your Holiness," Michelangelo told the pope.

"Why?" asked Pope Julius. "Because Apostles are poor," explained Michelangelo. The pope gave in without an argument.

"Do as you please," he grumbled and left Michelangelo to plan one of the most monumental art works in history.[46] Before he was finished with the Sistine Chapel ceiling, his great fresco scenes would include more than 340 figures.

PAINTING ON SCAFFOLDING

As Michelangelo designed the subject matter for his ceiling fresco, he created a large number of scenes and themes. He took stories from the book of Genesis, including the creation of the Sun and the Moon, and plants and animals. There would be scenes depicting the creation of Adam and the fall from the Garden of Eden. He wanted to depict images of Old Testament prophets and *sibyls*, female prophets. There would be scenes of the biblical flood and Noah. Figures from the Scriptures who were the "ancestors of Christ" were to be included— such as Moses, Jesse, David, Esther, and Judith. In his final plan, Michelangelo placed the more grue- some, sometimes bloody, chapters of Jewish biblical

A detail of God's and Adam's hands is shown here, from the Creation of Adam. This was one of the many biblical images Michelangelo included in his massive fresco on the ceiling of the Sistine Chapel.

history in the ceiling's corners. These included the boy David chopping off Goliath's head with a sword; Judith holding up the bloody head of her enemy, Holofernes; snakes biting the children of Israel in the desert; and the crucifixion of Haman, Queen Esther's enemy.

Michelangelo intended to paint a biblical spectacle based on salvation. From the Old Testament, he would show the salvation of the nation of Israel through Moses. Through the "ancestors," he would remind all viewers of his grand painting of the salvation of the world through Jesus Christ. Before he was finished designing his scenes for the chapel's ceiling, his plans led him to decide to continue painting down onto the walls, as well. The creative imagination of Michelangelo, it appears, was even larger than the ceiling of the Sistine Chapel.

Michelangelo began the work on the Sistine Chapel vault in early May 1508. It would preoccupy him for the next four years. Painting the ceiling of the Sistine Chapel presented special problems to Michelangelo, from the beginning. There were problems with the surface he was painting on and problems with the scaffolding he had for support while he painted. Michelangelo had very little experience painting frescoes, but his pride led him to refuse the help of experienced fresco painters. The Florentine artist chose, instead, to lock himself inside the chapel with a few workers and assistants, to paint the giant mural complex himself. He allowed no visitors, except by special permission, including the pope.

One of his first problems was with the scaffolding. Pope Julius had ordered Bramante to put up wooden frames for Michelangelo to stand on while he painted. Bramante had chosen to have holes drilled into the ceiling and to have the scaffolding hung from a large number of ropes. Michelangelo questioned Bramante, asking him how he would fill the holes after the scaffolding was taken down. The architect's answer, "We'll think of it when the time comes."[47]

When Michelangelo complained to Pope Julius, the pope ordered Michelangelo to set up the scaffolding in his own way. The Florentine sculptor had men build scaffolding from the floor upward, a complex framework of wooden beams and platforms, using no ropes at all. (Michelangelo gave Bramante's ropes to a poor carpenter, who sold them and made enough money to provide a dowry for his daughter, which allowed her to get married.) As for Bramante, he later copied Michelangelo's scaffolding system and used it to complete the work on St. Peter's.

Michelangelo had barely begun painting "when the work began to throw out mold to such an extent that the figures could hardly be seen through it."[48] He tried to get out of completing the project, telling the pope that he had already failed, but Pope Julius called in Sangallo to look at the ceiling. Sangallo explained to Michelangelo that he had put the plaster on too wet and that water was oozing to the surface of his fresco, causing the mold. The mold caused him to have to scrape off some of his early painting and begin again.

THE SUFFERING ARTIST

In addition to technical problems, Michelangelo had problems with the pope. Pope Julius let many months go by without paying Michelangelo anything, yet, the pope was always trying to get a glimpse at the progress of the work. According to Michelangelo biographer Condivi:

> While he was painting, Pope Julius used often-
> times to go and see the work, climbing by a
> ladder, while Michelangelo gave him a hand to
> help him on to the platform. One day the Pope
> asked him, as he had often done, when he
> would finish and Michelangelo answered,

according to his custom, "When I can." The Pope, who was irritable, struck him with his staff, saying, "When I can, when I can!" Michelangelo rushed home and began to make his preparations to leave Rome. The Pope sent hurriedly after him an amiable young man . . .

Michelangelo's Family Problems

While working on the ceiling of the Sistine Chapel, Michelangelo faced many problems and distractions. He dealt with everything from the pope's temper to a serious outbreak of mold on the painting's surface, but Michelangelo faced other problems in his personal life, as well. His family often served as his most constant distraction.

During the years he lived in Bologna and Rome, Michelangelo gave financial support and personal advice to several of his family members. He bought two farms for his father to help support him. He helped provide money to set up two of his brothers, Buonarroto and Giansimone, in business as wool merchants. In fact, Michelangelo spent much of the money he received from his art projects trying to provide better lives for his family members.

who gave Michelangelo 500 ducats . . . and apologized for Julius II. Michelangelo accepted the excuses.[49]

The very next day, however, Michelangelo and Pope Julius were arguing again as two frustrated

Michelangelo worried about his family constantly. When he received a letter about one of his brothers falling sick, he sent his own letter in response that same day. "I have a letter of yours this morning . . . which continues to distress me very much, learning as I do that Buonarroto is ill."[*] He became most worried for his family in Florence during the summer of 1512 as he was finishing the chapel ceiling project. An Italian army was advancing toward Florence. Michelangelo wrote to his brother Buonarroto, begging him to leave the city "with all the family and with all his money as well."[**] Ironically, the army was a papal force, under the command of Michelangelo's patron, Julius II.

[*] Linda Murray, *Michelangelo: His Life, Work and Times*. New York: Thames and Hudson, 1984, p. 62.
[**] Charles H. Morgan, *The Life of Michelangelo*. New York: Reynal & Company, 1966, p. 103.

rivals. The pope, in fact, even threatened to toss Michelangelo off the scaffolding. During the four years that Michelangelo worked on the ceiling, he experienced unhappiness, dissatisfaction, and poverty. In a letter he wrote to his father in January 1509, he said:

> I am attending to work as much as I can. . . . I don't have a penny. So I cannot be robbed. . . . I am unhappy and not in too good health staying here, and with a great deal of work, no instructions, and no money. But I have good hopes God will help me.[50]

The overworked artist was often depressed. Writing to his brother Buonarroto, he claimed, "I live here in great toil and great weariness of body, and have no friends of any kind and don't want any, and haven't the time to eat what I need. . . ."[51]

Sometimes while painting the Sistine Chapel, Michelangelo faced extreme physical challenges. On one occasion, he slipped from his scaffold and tumbled down a considerable distance, hurting himself severely. His biographer Vasari described some of his physical difficulties while working on scaffolding in the chapel:

> He executed the frescoes in great discomfort, having to work with his face looking upward, which impaired his sight so badly that he could not read or look at drawings save with his head turned backwards: and this lasted for several months afterward.[52]

While Michelangelo complained of his discomfort in private letters to family and friends, he also wrote poetry such as the following, describing his difficulties:

> *I've got myself a goitre [a swelling in the neck]*
> * from the strain*
> *As water gives the cats in Lombardy,*
> *Or maybe it's in some other country.*
> *My stomach's pushed by force beneath my chin,*
> *My beard towards heaven, and my brain I feel*
> *Is shoved upon my nape, and my breast is like a Harpy,*
> *And the brush, ever over my face*
> *Makes a rich pavement with its droppings. . .*

In front of me my skin is stretched
And to bend it, folds itself behind
And stretches like a Syrian bow.
Thus, wrongheaded and strange
Emerge the judgments that the mind brings forth,
In that no good shot comes from a crooked gun.
My painting, when I'm dead, defend it Giovanni,
And my Honour too, since I am not in a good place,
And am not a painter either.[53]

The great Florentine artist actually worked on his ceiling masterpiece in two separate blocks of time. In addition, he usually did not paint during the two coldest months of each winter. The first productive period lasted from 1508 through 1509. During late 1510, the scaffolding had to be moved beneath the second half of the chapel. This gave Michelangelo time to make two trips outside Rome. The first trip took place in September, and the second in December. By February 1511, he was back to work. He did not stop until he completed the ceiling, in October 1512.

On November 1, 1512—All Saints' Day—Pope Julius sat on the papal throne in the Sistine Chapel, as visitors were allowed to come and view the finished frescoes on the chapel's ceiling. The pope had already said Mass in the chapel as early as August 1511, but the people of Rome crowded into the Vatican hall and stared with wonder at the master-piece Michelangelo had labored over for so long. As the biographer Condivi wrote, Michelangelo's magnificent painting placed the Florentine artist "above the reach of envy."[54] Michelangelo had created a painted masterpiece, and he was only 37 years old. As for Pope Julius, on that November day, he felt ill, and knew his famous iron strength was leaving him. By Christmas, he could not eat and his sleep was fitful. By late February 1513, just four months after Michelangelo tore down the scaffold and uncovered the ceiling of the Sistine Chapel for the world to see, Pope Julius II died, probably from malaria.

Test Your Knowledge

1 What happened to the *Julius the Colossus*?
   a. It was hailed as Michelangelo's greatest work.
   b. It was moved to a museum in Florence.
   c. It was torn down, scrapped, and melted.
   d. It was moved to St. Peter's Cathedral.

2 Before Michelangelo began work on the Sistine
   Chapel fresco, how was the ceiling painted?
   a. Pale blue with a scattering of gold stars
   b. With clouds and angels
   c. With an image of the Crucifixion
   d. It was not painted at all.

3 What challenge did Michelangelo face in completing the Sistine Chapel fresco?
   a. The ceiling was vaulted (curved).
   b. The ceiling measured over 6,000 square feet.
   c. Mold growing on the wet plaster damaged
      his early efforts.
   d. All of the above

4 Where did Michelangelo get his inspiration for
   the figures depicted in the Sistine Chapel
   fresco?
   a. From Pope Julius II
   b. From other painters
   c. From the book of Genesis
   d. From his earlier work as a sculptor

5 How long did it take Michelangelo to complete the Sistine Chapel fresco?

a. Four years

b. Six months

c. One year

d. A lifetime

ANSWERS: 1. c; 2. a; 3. d; 4. c; 5. a

Endless Projects

No one really knows how Michelangelo felt when Pope Julius II died. The two men had always had a difficult relationship, but they were alike in many ways. Both men were strong and forceful, each with a different artistic vision. The biographer Vasari wrote, "Michelangelo knew the Pope and was, after all, much attached to him."[55] While the Florentine artist probably felt sadness at the pontiff's passing, he also knew that his long abandoned tomb project would be revived. He could finally, after four years of painting hundreds of figures on the ceiling of the Sistine Chapel, return to his favorite art form—sculpture.

Indeed, Michelangelo did work on Pope Julius II's tomb, from 1513 to 1516. Not long after the pope's death, the artist signed a new agreement with Pope Julius's heirs, and made his way back to Florence. As for the new pope, Michelangelo knew him well. He was Giovanni de' Medici, who became Pope Leo X. He was the first Florentine to be elected pope, and Michelangelo had known him as a boy, when he lived with the Medicis, under Lorenzo de' Medici's guidance. With the rise of Giovanni de' Medici to the papal throne, the Medici family was, once again, in power—this time over both Florence and Rome.

During these years, Michelangelo worked almost without interruption, a significant change from his days working for Pope Julius, who had been constantly underfoot. He carved three of his most important marble works during these years, including

The Dying Slave, The Rebellious Slave, and the seated statue of *Moses*. All three were supposed to be included in the design of Pope Julius's tomb. By the time the project was actually completed in its final form, however, only *Moses* was included.

The tomb would become a great problem for Michelangelo. The biographer Condivi referred to Michelangelo's 1513 return to the project as follows: "Michelangelo again embarked upon the tragedy of the tomb."[56] It haunted him for more than 40 years— from 1505 to 1545—as the monumental work remained unfinished all that time. When the tomb was finally built, it was a much smaller work than the ambitious Michelangelo had originally planned. For much of the time between 1516 and 1534, Michelangelo's talents were drained on gigantic projects "that never saw the light of day."[57]

For three years, he labored on the tomb. During that time, the new pontiff, Pope Leo X, allowed Michelangelo to focus on Pope Julius's monument, but the cost became an issue with the new pope. Jealousy may also have entered into the picture. Pope Leo X may have finally grown tired of his best sculptor creating a grand work in the name of

Following the death of Pope Julius in February 1513, Michelangelo worked on several marble sculptures. *The Dying Slave*, shown here, was supposed to be part of the design for Pope Julius's tomb, but it was not included in the finished tomb.

another pope. By 1515, he began pulling Michelangelo away to other projects of his choosing. That summer, the Florentine artist wrote a letter to his father. "This summer I must make a great effort to finish this work [on the tomb] . . . because I think that I shall soon have to enter the service of the Pope."[58] He was right. He did not, however, finish the tomb. It did not mark the end of his work on Pope Julius's tomb. Instead it was just one more postponement. The tomb project would, in fact, not be completed until 1547, some 42 years after Michelangelo began work on it.

THE FACADE OF SAN LORENZO

Pope Leo X lured Michelangelo away from Pope Julius's tomb by placing him in charge of creating a new, monumental project. He was to design the facade of San Lorenzo, the Medici church in Florence. In his imagination, Michelangelo had great plans. "I intend to make of this facade of San Lorenzo . . . a mirror for architecture and sculpture for all Italy. . . I will complete the work in six years."[59] "With God's help, I will create the finest work in all Italy."[60] The contract for the San Lorenzo facade was signed on January 19, 1518, and

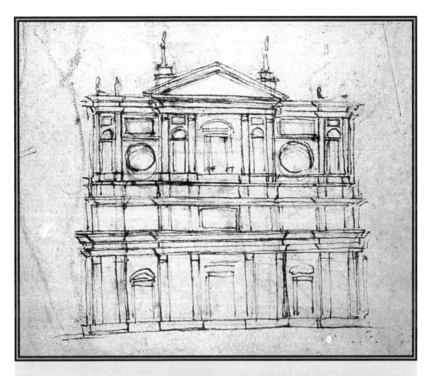

Pope Leo X hired Michelangelo to design the facade of San Lorenzo, the Medici church in Florence. One of Michelangelo's sketches of the facade is shown here.

the stated time for Michelangelo to complete the project was eight years.

With great expectations for his Medici project, Michelangelo visited several marble quarries. The blocks he had cut out of the quarries were huge. He constructed a large wooden model of his planned facade, intending to recreate it all from marble. In the meantime, the heirs of Pope Julius II appealed to Michelangelo to keep working on the pontiff's tomb. Incredibly, he signed a new contract for a smaller version of the tomb that would require him to work on both projects at the same time, one in Florence, and the other in Rome. Michelangelo had become greedy.

At one point, Pope Leo X banned Michelangelo from working on Pope Julius's tomb altogether. Caught between projects, Michelangelo made little progress on either. By 1520, Pope Leo X cancelled the great marble facade the Florentine sculptor had always envisioned for Pope Julius's tomb. Michelangelo became extremely bitter at the actions taken by Pope Leo. He wrote to the pope, the second longest letter of his life, noting his personal sacrifice on the project that had suddenly been taken from him, supposedly, because of its cost:

> I am not charging to the Pope's account the fact that I have been ruined over the said work at San Lorenzo . . . I am not charging to his account the enormous insult of having been brought here to execute the said work and then having it taken away from. . . . I am not charging to his account.[61]

Although Michelangelo complained bitterly about Pope Leo's decision, the pope would not change his mind. Instead Pope Leo X placed Michelangelo on two other projects. He was commissioned to build a Medici mausoleum at San Lorenzo, and he would construct the Laurentian Library. The library was to house the fabulous collection of Medici books and manuscripts. The mausoleum project was spurred on by the deaths of two members of the Medici family—Giuliano, brother to Leo X, and Lorenzo de' Medici. In the meantime, Pope Leo died in 1521, and a new pope, his cousin, Giulio de' Medici, was elected as Pope Clement VII. Michelangelo had also known him as a boy. He would become one of Michelangelo's favorite patrons, proving to be patient and sensitive.

The two men blazed artistic trails together, as they worked on projects that became some of Michelangelo's most acclaimed. For almost 20 years, from 1516 to 1534, Michelangelo worked on commissions he received from the Medicis. Working at San Lorenzo, his project took on a grand scale. More than 300 workers and artisans assisted Michelangelo on the massive works. He chose men he knew, for the most part, many of them friends and seasoned professional artists. Records exist of the names—nicknames, really—of many of these hand-picked associates of Michelangelo's: "Stick," "Dolt," "Fats," "Lefty," "Goose," "Woodpecker," "Thief," "Porcupine," "She-Cat," "the Fly," "Stumpy," "the Turk," "the Little Liar," "the Basket," and "Gloomy." During many of these years, Michelangelo, who turned 50 in 1525, worked as painter, sculptor, and architect, as well as business manager.

During the 1520s, Michelangelo and his vast crew of assistants and artisans did make progress on the Medici Chapel at San Lorenzo and the family library. There were serious interruptions, however. In the spring of 1527, foreign troops under Roman Emperor Charles V, invaded Italy and ransacked the city of Rome. Michelangelo fled the city, as did the pope and his family. This invasion allowed Florence to attempt to throw off Medici rule, and Michelangelo, who loved liberty, sided with the rebels and the Florentine Republic. At one point, the rebels placed Michelangelo in charge of designing fortifications for the city. For his part, Michelangelo, a loyal Florentine, designed and directed the erection of

In addition to the Medici Chapel in San Lorenzo, Michelangelo also worked on the Medici family library. The reading room of the library is shown here.

massive defenses around the city, allowing Florence to hold out for ten months during a siege laid by Medici supporters. (By 1529, the pope and Emperor Charles had come to an agreement, and the Medici family was back in power the following year.)

Florence finally fell on August 12, 1530. Fortunately for Michelangelo, Pope Clement forgave him for supporting Florence during these years, and instructed him to take up work on the project at San Lorenzo. Michelangelo, however, had, by then, lost much of his sense of commitment to the Medici church project. Florence fell under the leadership of a tyrannical strongman, which drove Michelangelo away from the city and countryside of his youth and back to Rome. His brother Buonarroto had died of the plague in 1527, and his father died in 1531. In 1534, he left Florence, never to return again. For the next 30 years of his life, he stayed in Rome, exiled from his homeland. Just two days after Michelangelo arrived in Rome, on September 23, Pope Clement died.

As always, Rome still had its lures for Michelangelo. That same year, a new pope came to power, Paul III, who would remain the head of the Roman Catholic Church for 15 years. As with Pope Clement, he and Michelangelo had a mutual respect for one another. During his entire reign, Pope Paul III kept Michelangelo busy on a multitude of projects. One of the first projects he assigned to the exiled Florentine was to paint the wall behind the altar of the Sistine Chapel, but Michelangelo still wanted to continue work on the tomb of Pope Julius II. When the artist protested, unwilling to take up another massive painting project, the pope delivered a harsh response, saying, "I have nursed this ambition for thirty years, and now that I'm pope am I not to have it satisfied? . . . I'm determined to have you in my service, no matter what."[62]

In 1535, to ensure Michelangelo's loyalty, Pope Paul appointed him "Artist, Chief Architect, Sculptor and Painter to the Apostolic Palace," and granted him an annual salary of 1,200 gold ducats. Michelangelo, in return, accepted the task of decorating the Sistine Chapel. While painting the altar wall had not been Michelangelo's choice, he was thrilled to be able to replace the existing altar murals, which had been painted earlier by an artist named Perugino. He was a painter Michelangelo did not like. That year, Michelangelo turned 60 years old. Several of his old Renaissance rivals were already dead. Leonardo da Vinci had died in 1519, and the youthful artists Raphael and Bramante had died the following year. Michelangelo was the undisputed living master of the Italian Renaissance.

Test Your Knowledge

1 What did Michelangelo do after the death of
Pope Julius II?
a. He retired.
b. He worked tirelessly on new sculptures.
c. He took a vacation in Spain.
d. He began to teach at Italy's art academies.

2 Michelangelo's work during this time included
a. *Moses.*
b. *The Dying Slave.*
c. *The Rebellious Slave.*
d. all of the above.

3 What reason did Pope Leo X give Michelangelo
for stopping work on the tomb of Pope Julius?
a. The project had become too expensive.
b. He was jealous of Pope Julius.
c. He wanted Michelangelo to return to
painting.
d. He didn't like the quality of the stone
the artist was using.

4 Pope Clement VII was
a. Michelangelo's childhood friend.
b. patient and sensitive about Michelangelo's
work.
c. one of Michelangelo's greatest patrons.
d. all of the above.

5 While working at San Lorenzo, Michelangelo employed how many artisans and assistants?

a. 50

b. 1,000

c. Over 300

d. 12

ANSWERS: 1. b; 2. d; 3. a; 4. d; 5. c

The Last Judgment

From 1536 until 1541, Michelangelo threw himself into painting a vast mural titled *The Last Judgment*. The altar wall measured approximately 50 feet high and 40 feet wide, but the space to be decorated was much smaller than the chapel ceiling, which Michelangelo had completed in less than four years. The Florentine artist was getting older. Despite his age, however, he worked with tremendous energy, again painting from a scaffold erected in the Sistine Chapel. At one point, he fell from the scaffolding and seriously injured his leg, but the accident did not stop his progress.

Michelangelo's *Last Judgment* was just as heavily populated as his ceiling frescoes, but was not nearly as complicated in structure and style. Dozens and dozens of people were included in the painting, but rather than including many people from the pages of the Bible, Michelangelo's wall painting was divided into two halves. Its subjects fell into one of two groups— "the saved," who were bound for heaven, and "the lost," who were being condemned to hell. The painting's figures included horned demons pulling various types of sinners down. There were serpents and wild-eyed satanic creatures, including Charon, the ancient Roman god of the underworld. Horror was frozen on the faces of many of those who found themselves plunged into the realm of the condemned.

Presiding over the entire painting, however, Michelangelo placed the risen Christ with the Virgin Mary at his right hand. He did not paint the common model of a Renaissance Jesus. Instead, Jesus was young, clean shaven, and muscular, a handsome figure who was seen as the answer to the prayers of millions of the faithful. Angels lifted them up to the heavenly realms. The saved were made up of various saints, including St. Lawrence, St. Bartholomew, and others depicted by Michelangelo. Bartholomew was shown near the foot of the Son of God, holding the drooping remains of his skin. (According to tradition, Bartholomew had been skinned alive with a knife.) The face of the flayed skin was a self-portrait of Michelangelo.

Michelangelo's *Last Judgment* was completed in 1541 and unveiled on October 31, All Saints Eve, 29 years to the day from the time his Sistine Chapel ceiling frescoes had been revealed to the public. His latest project was a success, but was not without controversy. Some were critical of the number of nude figures, including that of Christ. A few years after the mural was completed, another pope decided to cover up some of the exposed body parts. He hired one of Michelangelo's assistants, Daniele da Volterra, to drape cloth here and there on various private parts, work which earned Volterra the nickname, "Daniele the Breeches Maker." Despite such problems, *The Last Judgment* was another masterpiece for Michelangelo. As biographer Vasari described the work, *The Last Judgment* "marvelously portrayed all the emotions that mankind can experience. . . . Michelangelo's figures reveal thoughts and emotions that only he has known how to express."[63]

THE FINAL YEARS

By 1541, Michelangelo had become an old man. He was 66 years old, but he had not stopped working. Within months of finishing *The Last Judgment*, he began working on two frescoes for the Pauline Chapel in the Vatican—*The Conversation of St. Paul* and *The Crucifixion of St. Peter*. The paintings took eight years to complete. During that time, Pope Paul appointed Michelangelo as architect-in-chief of St. Peter's, even as the aged Florentine artist worked on other projects, including those for the Farnese family palace and rebuilding of Rome's fortifications. (Pope Paul III was a member of the Farnese family.) Michelangelo carved a work called *The Deposition,* depicting Jesus being taken down from the cross. The sculpture included the follower of Christ named Nicodemus, as well as the Virgin

Mary. Even in his later years, Michelangelo continued to sculpt marble with his aged hands. Vasari
stated, "His genius and his strength alike needed the
act of creation. . . . He attacked a block of marble,
cutting out of it four figures larger than life,
amongst them the dead Christ."[64] Despite his age,
he worked with marble

> with such fury one felt that the stone must shatter;
> he would break off big fragments, three or four
> inches thick, with a single blow, cutting them so
> close to the line, that if he had gone a hairs-
> breadth further, he risked losing everything.[65]

The old sculptor slept little, choosing to work day
and night. He attached a candle to his cap to help
him see while carving after a Roman sunset. The
work on *The Deposition* was never truly completed,
and Michelangelo continued to work on it for many
more years.

Additional popes came and went, but still
Michelangelo continued his work in Rome, with
each new pontiff reappointing the Florentine artist
as the chief architect of St. Peter's. Much of the work
was completed during the reign of Pope Pius IV,

With age, Michelangelo began to slow down. This marble bust, *Brutus*, was one of only three sculptures that Michelangelo completed in the last 30 years of his life.

between 1559 and 1565. Despite his best efforts, however, Michelangelo was slowing down with each passing year. During the last three decades of his life, he only completed three sculptures: the *Rachel* and the *Leah* for Pope Julius II's tomb and a marble bust, *Brutus.* In 1555, Michelangelo reached the age of 80, an incredible accomplishment in an era when most people did not even live to 40 years of age.

During his final years, he began to suffer physical problems, including kidney stones. He carved less, wrote more poetry, and shared more time with friends. In his faith, he became more optimistic than ever before, but in his art, he was still his worse critic. Just days before his death, he penned the following: "No one has full mastery / before reaching the end / of his art and his life."[66] He had seen a full and productive career that spanned more than 75 years, but still, as death approached, he did not feel he had accomplished enough or that his works were good enough.

By the time of his death, he had worked for nine popes. The end came in February 1564. On the twelfth day of the month, he spent the day chiseling away at his *Deposition,* which he had begun 15 years earlier. Two days later, he came down with a fever. Nonetheless, he went for a long horseback ride in the rain. For two more days, he fought against taking to his sickbed. He died on February 18, just two weeks short of his eighty-ninth birthday. Church officials wanted to bury him within St. Peter's, but Michelangelo had left instructions to his assistants "to return [me] to Florence when I am dead, since I was unable to return alive."[67] By March 10, 1564, his body was back in Florence, and was placed in the Santa Croce Church. There his coffin was opened to reveal Michelangelo dressed in black, including his hat and boots with spurs, as if ready to go somewhere.

For some, the spirit of the Renaissance died with Michelangelo. Certainly Italian art, indeed, the art of Europe, would never be the same or experience such an exciting and productive time of artistic creativity. The same year Michelangelo died, the great astronomer Galileo and the brilliant English playwright William Shakespeare were born. Europe was giving birth to a new age, but the shining spirit of Michelangelo would never be forgotten. Michelangelo is remembered in the pages of countless books and in his art, which today may be found from Florence to Rome, and beyond. He is remembered in the words of his biographer Vasari who said, "He made me astonished that the ancients are surpassed by the beauty and grace of what his divine genius has been able to achieve."[68]

Meanwhile, in the Rest of Europe. . .

Most people remember the Renaissance as a great period for the arts. It was in this world that Michelangelo lived for nearly 90 years, but there were many other things happening in Europe during the life of this remarkable artist. It was certainly a busy era, one that took Europeans places they had never gone before.

One of those places was America. When Michelangelo was still a teenager, another Italian named Christopher Columbus sailed west across the Atlantic Ocean in search of the riches and spices of the Orient. Instead he reached a world no European knew existed. European colonization of North America, Central America, and South America soon followed. Five years later, another European sea captain, Portuguese sailor Vasco da Gama, sailed around the southern tip of Africa, opening up a direct route to the wealth of the East. A generation later, the Spanish sailor Ferdinand Magellan's ships sailed completely around the earth. Suddenly the world seemed much larger to Europeans.

European technology was also changing during Michelangelo's lifetime. During the late 1400s, printing was experiencing a revolution with the development of the printing press and movable type. German printer Johann Gutenberg helped lead the way by publishing multiple copies of the Bible.

Christianity was also changing. By the early 1500s, a German theologian named Martin Luther was challenging the Roman Catholic Church and leading a movement that became known as the Reformation. The result was the establishment of Protestantism, as many new groups of Christian believers broke from Catholicism.

In the sciences, great minds were also making new discoveries. Near the end of Michelangelo's life, Polish astronomer Copernicus published a book in which he correctly stated the Sun was the center of our solar system, not Earth, as nearly everyone had believed for thousands of years.

Two other important books of the Renaissance were produced by a pair of fellow Italians during Michelangelo's later years. The books were *The Courtier,* by Baldassare Castiglione, and *The Prince*, by Niccolò Machiavelli. Both works presented the new ideal model of what a man ought to be in early sixteenth-century Europe. Castiglione presented the picture of the ideal Renaissance man, one who is well rounded and multitalented. Machiavelli's work presented a good leader as one who is both wise and virtuous, as well as self-interested and cunning.

The books were important works in their time. In fact, Emperor Charles V of the Holy Roman Empire only kept three books by his bedside—those by Castiglione and Machiavelli and the Bible.

Test Your Knowledge

1 Michelangelo took how long to complete
The Last Judgment?
a. Four years
b. One year
c. Six months
d. Twelve years

2 Which figure(s) did Michelangelo include in
The Last Judgment?
a. Horned demons
b. Charon, Roman ruler of the Underworld
c. The risen Christ
d. All of the above

3 What controversy surrounded *The Last Judgment?*
a. Some believed it was too expensive.
b. Some believed it was too large.
c. Some were offended by its depiction
of nudity.
d. Some thought it was not Michelangelo's
best work.

4 How many Popes commissioned Michelangelo's
work during the artist's lifetime?
a. Nine
b. Five
c. Three
d. Twelve

5 Looking back on his own work, Michelangelo considered himself

a. to have mastered his craft.

b. a legend.

c. still not sufficiently accomplished.

d. a failure.

ANSWERS: 1. a; 2. d; 3. c; 4. a; 5. c

1475 Michelangelo is born on March 6, in Caprese, Italy, near the city-state of Florence.

1483 Painter Raphael is born.

1488 Apprenticeship for Michelangelo begins in the workshop of master painter Ghirlandaio.

1489 Michelangelo is introduced into the household of strongman ruler Lorenzo de' Medici; he remains in the house of Lorenzo de' Medici until 1492.

1492 Lorenzo the Magnificent dies in Florence.

1494–1496 Michelangelo travels to Venice and Bologna and finally arrives in Rome during the summer of 1496.

1519 Michelangelo is commissioned to design and decorate the Medici Tombs; Leonardo da Vinci dies the same year

1498 Completion of Michelangelo's first sculpture, the *Pieta*

1475 Birth of Michelangelo

1475

1489 Introduction of Michelangelo into the house of the Medicis

1501 Michelangelo is commissioned to sculpt his *David* in marble for the Piazza della Signoria in Florence

1498 Michelangelo completes his first masterpiece sculpture, the *Pieta.*

1501 Michelangelo is commissioned to sculpt his *David* in marble for the Piazza della Signoria in Florence.

1503 Florence city leaders commission the sculpting of the *Twelve Apostles*; the project is later cancelled in 1505.

1504 Michelangelo paints the *Doni Tondo.*

1505 Back in Rome, Michelangelo is commissioned by Pope Julius II to design his tomb.

1508 In April, the Florentine artist is commissioned to begin decorating the ceiling of the Sistine Chapel; the frescoes

1534 Michelangelo creates early drawings for *The Last Judgment* on the altar wall of the Sistine Chapel; he completes the wall frescoes in the chapel by 1541

1564 Michelangelo dies on February 18

1570

1530 Fall of the Republic of Florence

1546 The pope appoints Michelangelo as the chief architect for the completion of St. Peter's in Rome

take four years to complete and are officially inaugurated on October 31, 1512.

1511   Vasari, one of Michelangelo's most important biographers, is born.

1513   Pope Leo X, the son of Lorenzo de' Medici, is elected.

1518   Michelangelo is commissioned to create the facade of the San Lorenzo Church, but the project is never completed.

1519   Michelangelo is commissioned to design and decorate the Medici Tombs; Leonardo da Vinci dies the same year.

1520   Michelangelo's younger rival, Raphael, dies.

1523   Clement VII (Giulio de' Medici) succeeds Adrian VI as pope.

1524   Michelangelo takes on the decoration of the Laurentian Library for the Medici family.

1527   Rome is sacked by imperial troops of Emperor Charles V; the Florentine Republic is reestablished, following the collapse of the house of Medici.

1529   Michelangelo is appointed to design fortifications for the city of Florence; before the year is over, he will flee the city into exile in Venice, only to return before year's end to Florence.

1530   The Republic of Florence falls.

1534   Pope Paul III is elected; Michelangelo creates early drawings for *The Last Judgment* on the altar wall of the Sistine Chapel; Michelangelo completes the wall frescoes in the chapel by 1541.

1537 Michelangelo sculpts *Brutus* bust for Cardinal Ridolfi.

1546 The pope appoints Michelangelo as the chief architect for the completion of St. Peter's in Rome.

1555 Michelangelo carves *The Deposition*, but the work remains unfinished through the rest of Michelangelo's life.

1557–1561 Michelangelo submits various models for St. Peter's to the pope.

1564 Michelangelo dies on February 18.

CHAPTER 2
The Artist's Youth

1. Gilles Neret, *Michelangelo: 1475–1564*. New York: Barnes & Noble Books, 2001, p. 13.

2. Howard Hibbard, *Michelangelo*. New York: Harper & Row, Publishers, 1974, p. 16.

3. Charles H. Morgan, *The Life of Michelangelo*. New York: Reynal & Company, 1966, p. 54.

4. William Wallace, *Michelangelo: The Complete Sculpture, Painting, Architecture*. New York: Hugh Luter Levin Associates, 1998, p. 13.

CHAPTER 3
Learning His Craft

5. Hibbard, *Michelangelo*, p. 20.

6. Ibid.

7. Ibid., p. 21.

8. Ibid., p. 22.

9. Neret, *Michelangelo: 1475–1564*, p. 15.

10. Wallace, *Michelangelo: The Complete Sculpture, Painting, Architecture*, p. 17.

11. Ibid.

12. Hibbard, *Michelangelo*, p. 38.

13. Ibid., p. 43.

CHAPTER 4
The Heart of a Sculptor

14. Robert Coughlan, *The World of Michelangelo: 1475–1564*. New York: Time Incorporated, 1966, p. 73.

15. Linda Murray, *Michelangelo: His Life, Work and Times*. New York: Thames and Hudson, 1984, p. 20.

16. Coughlan, *The World of Michelangelo: 1475–1564*, p. 74.

17. Ibid.

18. Anthony Hughes, *Michelangelo*. London: Phaidon Press Limited, 1997, p. 58.

19. Coughlan, *The World of Michelangelo: 1475–1564*, p. 85.

20. Ibid.

21. Giorgio Vasari, *Lives of the Most Eminent Painters, Sculptors, and Architects*. New York: The Modern Library, 1959, pp. 318–319.

22. Coughlan, *The World of Michelangelo: 1475–1564*, p. 85.

CHAPTER 5
The Stonecutter and the Shepherd Boy

23. Hibbard, *Michelangelo*, p. 52.

24. Morgan, *The Life of Michelangelo*, p. 61.

25. Vasari, *Lives of the Most Eminent Painters, Sculptors, and Architects*, p. 319.

26. Hibbard, *Michelangelo*, p. 56.

27. Coughlan, *The World of Michelangelo*, p. 87.

28. Ibid., p. 93.

29. Vasari, *Lives of the Most Eminent Painters, Sculptors, and Architects,* p. 319.

CHAPTER 6
The Pope and the Artist

30. Neret, *Michelangelo: 1475–1564,* p. 23.

31. Ibid.

32. Ibid.

33. Murray, *Michelangelo: His Life, Work and Times,* p. 50.

34. Coughlan, *The World of Michelangelo,* 107.

35. Ibid.

36. Hibbard, *Michelangelo,* p. 89.

37. Coughlan, *The World of Michelangelo,* p. 107.

38. Ibid.

39. Ibid., p. 109.

40. Ibid.

41. Ibid.

42. Neret, *Michelangelo: 1475–1564,* p. 24.

43. Murray, *Michelangelo: His Life, Work and Times,* p. 53.

CHAPTER 7
The Great Ceiling Painter

44. Hibbard, *Michelangelo,* p. 97.

45. Wallace, *Michelangelo: The Complete Sculpture, Painting, Architecture,* p. 21.

46. Rolf Schott, *Michelangelo.* New York: Tudor Publishing Company, 1963, p. 58.

47. Murray, *Michelangelo: His Life, Work and Times,* p. 55.

48. Coughlan, *The World of Michelangelo,* p. 113.

49. Ibid.

50. Hibbard, *Michelangelo,* p. 118.

51. Ibid., p. 119.

52. Murray, *Michelangelo: His Life, Work and Times,* p. 67.

53. Ibid.

54. Coughlan, *The World of Michelangelo,* p. 113.

CHAPTER 8
Endless Projects

55. Coughlan, *The World of Michelangelo,* p. 131.

56. Neret, *Michelangelo: 1475–1564,* p. 49.

57. Ibid.

58. Coughlan, *The World of Michelangelo,* p. 135.

59. Neret, *Michelangelo: 1475–1564,* p. 55.

60. Wallace, *Michelangelo: The Complete Sculpture, Painting, Architecture,* p. 22.

61. Ibid., p. 24.

62. Ibid., p. 27.

CHAPTER 9
The Last Judgment

63. Hibbard, *Michelangelo*, p. 254.

64. Neret, *Michelangelo: 1475–1564*, p. 85.

65. Ibid.

66. Wallace, *Michelangelo: The Complete Sculpture, Painting, Architecture*, p. 28.

67. Neret, *Michelangelo: 1475–1564*, p. 88.

68. Wallace, *Michelangelo: The Complete Sculpture, Painting, Architecture*, p. 29.

Clements, Robert J., ed. *Michelangelo: A Self-Portrait.* Englewood Cliffs, NJ: Prentice-Hall, 1963.

Coughlan, Robert. *The World of Michelangelo, 1475–1564.* New York: Time, 1966.

DeVecchi, Pierluigi. *Michelangelo: The Vatican Frescoes.* New York: Abbeville Press Publishers, 1996.

Gilbert, Creighton. *Michelangelo.* New York: McGraw-Hill Book Company, 1967.

Harris, Nathaniel. *Renaissance Art.* New York: Thomson Learning, 1994.

Hibbard, Howard. *Michelangelo.* New York: Harper & Row, Publishers, 1974.

Hughes, Anthony. *Michelangelo.* London: Phaidon Press Limited, 1997.

Morgan, Charles. *The Life of Michelangelo.* New York: Reynal & Company, 1966.

Murray, Linda. *Michelangelo: His Life, Work and Times.* New York: Thames and Hudson, 1984.

Neret, Gilles. *Michelangelo, 1475–1564.* New York: Barnes & Noble Books, 2001.

Schott, Rolf. *Michelangelo.* New York: Tudor Publishing Company, 1963.

Vasari, Giorgio. *Lives of the Most Eminent Painters, Sculptors, and Architects.* New York: The Modern Library, 1959.

Wallace, William E. *Michelangelo: The Complete Sculpture, Painting, Architecture.* New York: Hugh Lauter Levin Associates, 1998.

Wright, Susan. *The Renaissance: Masterpieces of Art and Architecture.* New York: Todtri Book Publishers, 1997.

Carvalho de Magalhaes, Roberto. *Michelangelo.* New York: Enchanted Lion Books, 2003.

Connolly, Sean. *Michelangelo.* Milwaukee: Gareth Stevens, 2003.

Cook, Diane. *Michelangelo: Renaissance Artist.* Philadelphia: Mason Crest Publishers, 2002.

Langley, Andrew. *Michelangelo.* Chicago: Raintree Publishers, 2003.

Rachlin, Ann. *Michelangelo.* New York: Barron's Educational Series, 1994.

Stanley, Diane. *Michelangelo.* New York: HarperCollins Children's, 2003.

Venezia, Mike. *Michelangelo.* New York: Scholastic Library Publishing, 1992.

Websites

Art Cyclopedia: Michelangelo Buonarroti
http://www.artcyclopedia.com/artists/michelangelo_buonarroti.html

Life of Michelangelo
http://easyweb.easynet.co.uk/giorgio.vasari/michel/michel.htm

Michelangelo Buonarroti, 1474–1564
http://www.michelangelo.com/buonarroti.html

Web Gallery of Art: Michelangelo Buonarroti
http://www.kfki.hu/~arthp/bio/m/michelan/biograph.html

Web Museum, Paris: Michelangelo
http://www.ibiblio.org/wm/paint/auth/michelangelo

Films

Michelangelo: Artist and Man. (Biography Series) A&E Home Video, 1994.

The Renaissance. (Just The Facts Learning Series) Goldhil Home Media International, 2001.

PICTURE CREDITS

Tim McNeese is a prolific author of books for elementary, middle- and high school, and college readers. He has published more than 70 books and educational materials over the past 20 years, on everything from Indian legends to the building of the Great Wall of China to a biography of President George W. Bush. McNeese is an Associate Professor of History at York College in York, Nebraska, where he is currently in his fourteenth year of teaching. Previously, he taught middle- and high school history, English, and journalism for 16 years. He is a graduate of York College (AA), Harding University (BA), and Southwest Missouri State University (BA, MA). His writing has earned him a citation in the library reference work, *Something About the Author*. His wife, Beverly, is an Assistant Professor of English at York College. They both love to travel. In 2003 and 2005, they hosted a college study trip for students along fifteen hundred miles of the Lewis and Clark Trail from eastern Nebraska to western Montana. They have two children, Noah and Summer. Readers may e-mail Professor McNeese at tdmcneese@york.edu.